The Owl
Was a Baker's Daughter

Marie-Louise von Franz, Honorary Patron

STUDIES IN JUNGIAN PSYCHOLOGY
BY JUNGIAN ANALYSTS

Daryl Sharp, General Editor

The Owl
Was a Baker's Daughter

Obesity, Anorexia Nervosa and
the Repressed Feminine

Marion Woodman

To the women who made this study possible

Canadian Cataloguing in Publication Data

Woodman, Marion
    The owl was a baker's daughter

(Studies in Jungian Psychology by Jungian analysts; 4)

Bibliography: p.
Includes index.

ISBN 0-919123-03-1

1. Obesity—Psychological aspects. 2. Anorexia
nervosa. 3. Women—Mental Health. 4. Jung, Carl Gustav,
1875-1961. I. Title. II. Series.

RC552.025W66   616.3'98   C80-094629-4

INNER CITY BOOKS
Box 1271, Station Q, Toronto, Canada M4T 2P4
(416) 927-0355

Honorary Patron: Marie-Louise von Franz.
Publisher and General Editor: Daryl Sharp.

INNER CITY BOOKS was founded in 1980 to promote the
understanding and practical application of the work of C.G. Jung.

Cover: Woodcut by Albrecht Durer (1508).
Frontispiece: Eryl Lauber and Ann Yeoman.

Glossary and Index by Daryl Sharp.

Printed and bound in Canada by
University of Toronto Press Incorporated

CONTENTS

Please see final pages for *Catalogue*

Stone Walls do not a Prison make,
Nor Iron bars a cage.

—Lovelace, "To Althea, from Prison"

Introduction

Fatness once carried happy connotations. People "laughed and grew fat"; the fortunate few "lived off the fat of the land"; the less fortunate many envied "the fat cat." In cultures less affluent than ours, the plump bride is still worth her weight in gold. In China and Japan, the person with the fat belly is respected and admired as being well grounded in himself. In Western society, however, the connotations have reversed. The 200-pounder has "a fat chance in a slim world" and the fat woman is ashamed to walk around "with her neurosis hanging out." Certainly, some women rejoice in their plumpness and experience no difficulties with their size. This book is not concerned with them. It is a study of the agonies of fatness and its psychic and somatic causes.

No magic or scientific formula has yet made any inroad on the growing obesity problem. I have documented my experimental findings as carefully as possible and quoted conversations verbatim in the hope of making conscious the inner world of the obese woman. Each is an individual, but each is obese. Consciousness will not always solve the problem, but it may make the suffering meaningful.

Many of the comments made by the obese women during the Association Experiment (detailed in Chapter I) could have been made by women of normal weight. Thinking women in 20th-century Western culture have much in common. Neurosis, however, manifests in an all-too-tangible form in the obese. This study focuses on the particular combination of factors that produce this particular symptom, shared by 40% of American women.

While thinking about a character who best personifies this particular combination, I repeatedly remembered one phrase from *Hamlet*: "As one incapable of her own distress." Then came the image of Ophelia singing to her flowers, floating downstream buoyed up by her billowing dress, borne on the waters which were destroying her. In that "sweet maid" buried in her courtier's garments I saw a princess sleeping in an obese body.

Ophelia was a father's daughter. Without a mother, she grew up in a court which demanded a certain code of behaviour. She fell in love

7

with a prince destined to be king. So long as their little paradise remained unthreatened by reality, Ophelia and Hamlet could love. But when "things rank and gross" suddenly destroyed their garden, and Lord Hamlet fell to perusal of her face, what he found there was a child who had not the inner resources to be true to her own self, least of all to him. When night followed day, she could do only as her father demanded—play out the role as his puppet—unconsciously betraying the woman she never found within herself and playing false to the man she believed she loved. She had no inner reality with which to respond to his masculine need. Where the woman's heart is piping her father's tune, "it is not, nor it cannot come to good."

Her father dead, her lover gone, Ophelia goes mad. In her insanity, she utters more truths than she is consciously capable of. Alone amidst the courtiers, she stands in bedraggled dress and weed-braided hair—a little bewitched bird—her eyes empty of everything but the demon that possesses her. Pathetically she cries:

> . . . . They say the owl was a baker's daughter. Lord, we know
> what we are, but know not what we may be.
> God be at your table! [1]

This is a reference to an old English legend:

> Our Saviour went into a baker's shop where they were baking and
> asked for some bread to eat. The mistress of the shop immediately put
> a piece of dough into the oven to bake for him; but was reprimanded
> by her daughter, who insisting that the piece of dough was too large,
> reduced it to a very small size. The dough, however, immediately afterwards
> began to swell, and presently became of a most enormous size.
> Whereupon, the baker's daughter cried out, "Heugh, heugh, heugh,"
> which owl-like noise probably induced our Saviour for her wickedness
> to transform her into that bird. [2]

Ironically, Ophelia is describing herself. Locked into her infantile needs, she fails to recognize the stranger. She cannot make the passover from childhood into womanhood; thus she is incapable of responding to Hamlet with the mature feeling which could put him in touch with his own feminine side and save him from his fatal self-alienation.

In another version of the legend it is Christmas Eve. The baker's daughter is so busy preparing the Christmas bread and putting her shop in order that she is angry with her naive father who wastes time feeding the beggar at the back door. Possessed by her own busyness and fantasies of the great day to come, she misses reality staring her in the face. The bread which she steals from the god swells "to a most enormous size"; the mystery which she rejects at the back door materializes into a monster at the front. Unable even to utter a human cry, she lets out three owl-like hoots and feels herself being transformed into a night bird. In Greece, the owl was Athena's bird, symbolizing her affinity with darkness. Athena too was a father's daughter, sprung from her father's forehead after he swallowed her pregnant mother.

Ophelia is a little walking owl, bewitched by her unconscious feminine, her father, and what "they say."[3] She never finds her own voice. She never finds her own body or her own feelings and therefore misses life and love in the here and now. Gradually the waters of the unconscious to which she is "native and indued" swallow her. Describing her death, Shakespeare says (through Queen Gertrude):

> There is a willow grows aslant a brook,
> That shows his hoar leaves in the glassy stream.
> . . . .
> There on the pendent boughs her coronet weeds
> Clamb'ring to hang, an envious sliver broke,
> When down her weedy trophies and herself
> Fell in the weeping brook. Her clothes spread wide
> And, mermaid-like, awhile they bore her up;
> Which time she chaunted snatches of old tunes,
> As one incapable of her own distress,
> Or like a creature native and indued
> Unto that element; but long it could not be
> Till that her garments, heavy with their drink,
> Pull'd the poor wretch from her melodious lay
> To muddy death.[4]

Every woman haunted by obesity knows the agony of looking into a mirror and seeing an owl staring back at her. If she dares to keep looking, she may even see her mermaid's tail. The split between her head and her body is destroying her life and she is powerless to break the spell. In this book, forty women and I have looked into the eyes of the owl as honestly as possible. Whatever light we found there is put forward in the following pages.

In essence I am suggesting that 20th-century women have been living for centuries in a male-oriented culture which has kept them unconscious of their own feminine principle. Now in their attempt to find their own place in a masculine world, they have unknowingly accepted male values—goal-oriented lives, compulsive drivenness, and concrete bread which fails to nourish their feminine mystery. Their unconscious femininity rebels and manifests in some somatic form. In this study, the Great Goddess either materializes in the obese or devours the anorexic. Her victim must come to grips with her femininity by dealing with the symptom. Only by discovering and loving the goddess lost within her own rejected body can a woman hear her own authentic voice. This book suggests practical ways of listening, and explores the meaning of the feminine as it "slouches towards Bethlehem to be born."[5]

CHAPTER I

EXPERIMENTAL BACKGROUND

> Where the realm of the complexes begins,
> the freedom of the ego comes to an end,
> for complexes are psychic agencies whose
> deepest nature is still unfathomed.
>
> —C.G. Jung, "A Review of the Complex
> Theory"

Modern research into obesity has proved that putting on weight is more than a simple matter of eating too much. Two individuals may eat exactly the same number of calories and lead an equally active life. One is fat, the other thin. The fat one may, in fact, be eating less and exercising more. The essential difference lies in the individual's capacity to metabolize the caloric intake. Behind any metabolic disturbance there may be both physiological and psychological causes.

Primary and Secondary Obesity

An important differentiation must be made at the outset. Some people seem to be "programmed" to be fat; others grow fat for diverse reasons. Endogenous or primary obesity develops from within; exogenous or secondary obesity requires overeating, i.e., is imposed from without. Excess calories are stored in adipose cells in the form of triglycerides. Anatomically, the triglycerides may be stored in pre-existing adipose cells, causing increased cell size, or by the formulation of new adipocytes, causing increased cell numbers. Early in life, cellular multiplication is the predominant factor responsible for the growth of adipose tissue, but later, cell number becomes fixed, and afterwards the adipose tissue expands or shrinks almost

11

exclusively by changes in fat cell size. It appears that the age at which the final cell number is reached and subsequently remains constant is around twenty years or earlier. In obesity there is a derangement of the orderly process of growth in adipose tissue both in cell size and cell number.[6]

Hypercellularity (increased number of cells) begins early in life, and may be genetically influenced. According to Beeson and McDermott's *Textbook of Medicine*:

> The localization of extreme deposits of fat, such as the massive adipose tissue over the buttocks of certain Bushmen, the so-called "Hottentot bustle," is an instance of genetically determined localized adiposity. This extreme example suggests that the number of adipose cells may be in part genetically determined and that the number and location of such cells or their precursors will determine in part the magnitude as well as the location of the obesity.[7]

The genetic influence is still debatable. However, there appear to be two periods in early life when hypercellularity is most likely to develop: very early, within the first few years, and later, around puberty. People with childhood obesity have the greatest increase in cell number and the most nearly normal cell size, while those who gain weight at puberty have smaller degrees of hypercellularity and larger fat cells. A second pattern of obesity is characterized by the presence of enlarged adipose cells but a normal number of them. This pattern begins in adult life and is usually mild to moderate in severity.

Weight reduction in all obese patients, regardless of age of onset or degree and duration of obesity, has been found to be achieved only through change in cell size. Cell number remains constant even where there is massive weight loss. Individuals obese from childhood may have three times as many fat cells as those of normal weight. This accounts for the fact that lifelong obese persons may lose weight, but almost inevitably regain it. The permanent fat cells are waiting to be refilled the moment will-power fades.

Moreover, there is some speculation that hypercellularity signals the hypothalamus to stimulate increased food intake.[8] According to this theory, the feeding centres control, and in turn are regulated by, the total amount of fat in the body. Thus hypercellularity would become a source of a permanent stimulus for excessive food intake. For some as yet undetermined reason, the "appestat" (the set point) in the obese person seems to be high and fixed, or high and rising, or strangely fluctuating. It seems logical, however, that where an obese woman is in intense psychological conflict, her homeostatic equilibrium will be disturbed, and while it may be artificially adjusted by diet and rigid self-control, it cannot be maintained permanently. Recent evidence, indeed, suggests that the body actually defends the adipose tissue mass.

> It is possible, that the hypothalamus defends different baselines in different individuals, maintaining whatever set point the individual is favoured with or saddled with. . . . This suggests that obesity, for some, is a "normal" or "ideal" body composition.[9]

These facts are crucial for any therapeutic situation involving obesity. Where hypercellularity is part of a woman's physical makeup, she may have to simply accept her body size as a "just so" story. This new attitude by itself may correct the constant fluctuations in weight. Secondary obesity, on the other hand, can be corrected through diet when psychic factors make diet desirable. Two additional points are worth remembering. First, the metabolic activity in the adipose tissue during the phase of active weight gain differs significantly from that observed once a steady state of obesity has been reached, and therefore significant accompanying mood changes may result.[10] Secondly, different types of food may be metabolized differently in fat people than in thin people, and no one diet is applicable to all. Each individual psyche has its own peculiar reality. As C.G. Jung comments:

> Despite the advances in organic chemistry, we are still very far from being able to explain consciousness as a biochemical process. On the contrary, we have to admit that the chemical laws do not even explain the selective process of food assimilation, let alone the self-regulation and self-preservation of the organism. Whatever the reality of the psyche may be, it seems to coincide with the reality of life and at the same time to have a connection with the formal laws governing the inorganic world.[11]

The interrelatedness of psyche and soma implied by this statement is developed in more detail in Chapter II.

C.G. Jung's Association Experiment

In his early career, Jung developed an empirical method of detecting what he subsequently called *feeling-toned complexes*. At first he simply elicited a series of spontaneous responses to a number of chosen stimulus words, attempting to establish the average speed and quality of the responses. He discovered, however, that more important than the reaction time was the way in which the method was *disturbed* by the autonomous behaviour of the psyche. He realized that it was not possible to investigate isolated psychic processes, and thus discovered the feeling-toned complexes which had always been registered before as failures to react. He defined the complex as follows:

> It is the *image* of a certain psychic situation which is strongly accentu-
> ated emotionally and is, moreover, incompatible with the habitual
> attitude of consciousness. This image has a powerful inner coherence, it
> has its own wholeness and, in addition, a relatively high degree of au-
> tonomy, so that it is subject to the control of the conscious mind to
> only a limited extent, and therefore behaves like an animated foreign
> body in the sphere of consciousness. The complex can usually be sup-
> pressed with an effort of the will, but not argued out of existence, and
> at the first suitable opportunity it reappears in all its original strength.[12]

Jung further pointed out that an outward situation may release a psychic process in which certain contents gather together and pre-pare for action. This he called a "constellation"; this is an automatic process which the individual cannot control. "The constellated con-tents are definite complexes possessing their own specific energy."[13] In the experimental situation, the complexes provoke disturbed re-actions, the most frequent being delayed reaction time. An active complex puts us momentarily under a spell of compulsive thinking and acting. Jung felt "moderately certain" that complexes were "splinter psyches" which appear in personified form in our dreams when there is no inhibiting consciousness to suppress them. Their origin is frequently a trauma or an emotional shock that splits off a part of the psyche. One of the commonest causes is a moral conflict in which the individual has not been able to affirm the whole of his nature. "This impossibility presupposes a direct split, no matter whether the conscious mind is aware of it or not."[14]

The more unconscious the individual is, the greater autonomy the complex has, even to the point where it may assimilate the ego, the result being a momentary alteration of personality known as "identi-fication with the complex." In the Middle Ages, this was called pos-session or bewitchment. "The *via regia* to the unconscious, how-ever," said Jung, "is not the dream, as [Freud] thought, but the complex, which is the architect of dreams and of symptoms."[15]

As the Association Experiment is conducted today, the volunteer is given a simple stimulus word to which he or she is asked to react with a single word. A prepared list of 100 words is used; each re-

sponse is accurately timed with a stopwatch and emotional disturbances are noted. Having completed the list, the volunteer is then
asked to repeat the original response to each word. The experiment-
er immediately assesses retarded reactions, failure of memory, per-
severation, emotional responses, etc., and asks the volunteer to
further associate to the original words showing disturbed reactions.
A careful analysis of the areas of disturbance and the associated comments makes possible a fairly accurate quantitative and qualitative
evaluation of the complexes.

The Association Experiment and Obesity

In an effort to understand the psychic dynamics behind obesity, I
conducted Jung's Association Experiment with twenty obese women.
(I chose to work with women only, because after conducting the experiment with three obese men I recognized that their problems
were very different, deserving a separate study.) The experiments
were carried out individually in the manner described above, each
one taking from two to four hours. Certain areas of fear and resistance were immediately evident in all twenty experiments. Some
words invariably caused hesitation and emotional distress. The following are a few examples listed with several typical responses:

try:	harder, fail, again
hunger:	pain, empty, longing, lump, poor, fear
plum:	fatness, round, plump, pudding
beat:	fight, kill, murder, hit
wait:	heavy, gain, fat, control, balloon, me
evil:	spirit, Satan, death, darkness, woman, me
choice:	none, blank, where?
swim:	water, drown, fear, cold, sink, fish

In several cases, these words or those immediately following were
not remembered in the memory part of the test. The sense of failure
is apparent in the resigned response to *try* and *choice*; the food complex appears in response to *hunger, plum, wait*; aggression lies behind the delayed response to *beat* (none heard this as beet); fear of
the unconscious may be hidden behind the responses to *evil* and
swim. These conclusions are based on memory failure, retarded response, emotional reaction, and additional factors not necessarily
apparent in the words themselves.

Where groups of words caused problems, these were considered
as a unit, e.g., angry, despise, nasty, beat, evil, insult. Where there

was any kind of disturbed response, I asked the woman to associate freely to that word. Usually she did so with considerable affect. As she talked I wrote down her comments verbatim. Samples of these appear later in this chapter.

Having completed the twenty experiments, I evaluated the data looking for patterns of response, focussing on repetitive themes, thus determining the areas in which complexes were active (Tables 1 and 2, column 1, pages 18 and 19). Their remarks were classified either by their direct statements or their implications. (My choice of categories in interpreting the comments is of course to some extent subjective.)

In order to discover whether there was any significant difference in the psychic dynamics of the obese and those of normal weight, I conducted another series of experiments with twenty controls. These were carried out in exactly the same way, with one difference. At the conclusion of each experiment, I told the subject what I was investigating and asked her to answer a series of questions assembled from the data of the obese volunteers. Without these questions there would have been no basis for contrast in the food categories, because food as a dominating factor was never mentioned by any of the controls. Significantly, the questions were often incongruous to them. Invariably, where the extremes of the eating disorder appeared in the questions, the controls had to stop to consider what the question could possibly mean.

The questions to the controls were as follows:

1. Were you fat as a child? At puberty? Were either of your parents fat?
2. Do you ever eat or refuse to eat in order to gain attention?
3. Do you eat when you are depressed? When anxious?
4. Do you eat when you cannot express your anger?
5. Do you ever eat to replace sexuality?
6. Would you find any satisfaction in stealing food?
7. Would you ever think of rewarding your body by giving it food?
8. Would you ever become so angry at your body that you would punish it by overeating foods that it could not digest?
9. Would you ever think of fasting to reward your body?
10. Would you ever think of fasting to punish your body?
11. Are you ever angry at yourself because of your body?
12. Are you ever angry at Fate because of your body?
13. How many calories a day can you eat without gaining weight?
14. Do you feel your body is properly utilizing the food you eat?
15. Do you have any chronic physical problems associated with food or sexuality?

The data assembled from the experiments and answers of the twenty controls are compiled in Tables 1 and 2, column 2, pages 18 and 19. Other relevant facts concerning the two groups are documented in Table 3, page 37.

In compiling the data for Tables 1 and 2, i.e., in assessing the intensity of the responses, I had to make a subjective appraisal based on the statements or the emotional reactions. For instance, "hypersensitivity" (Table 1, row 34) is relative, but where a life is controlled by fear of other people's reactions and one's own physical reaction to emotional pain, hypersensitivity seemed to be the right word. Similarly, "perfectionist" (Table 1, row 31) in this study refers to a person who will drive herself to exhaustion in an effort to meet her own inner needs and standards. This is complicated by the fact that many of these women are outstanding, creatively and artistically. In this area, it is very difficult to separate the power drive from the inner need for creative perfection. (The role of the creative woman in a patriarchal culture is one of the underlying themes of this book.) All of the participants were intelligent; "above average intelligence" (Table 1, row 33) in this group means that they were outstanding students throughout their educational years in terms of marks and scholarships.

My feeling is that weight problems are related to psychological typology. Certainly intuitives seem to be more prone to eating disorders, and sensation types less so, but this whole question merits a study in itself.[16]

In order to elucidate the tabulated data, comments as they were made by the obese during the experiments are quoted below verbatim. Where certain themes were constantly repeated, I chose statements which most succinctly summarized the attitude. (These are listed at random in order to protect the anonymity of the participants.)

There must, of course, be overlapping among the complexes and certain undercurrents are always present. For example, the influence of the "negative animus" (one form of bewitchment) contaminates the entire personality. Repeatedly in the comments we hear a voice separating the woman from her true feelings, filling her mouth with worn-out opinions, sapping her energy in attempting to please others or her own introjected parents. From childhood, the rigidity of the mother together with the perfectionist standards of the father have caused the child to swallow her fear and resentment, stifling the emo-

ROW	COMPLEXES and PERSONALITY TRAITS	Column 1 Obese (of 20)	Column 2 Controls (of 20)
1	Negative Mother	16	5
2	Positive Mother	4	15
3	Identification with Mother	6	12
4	Mother Dominated Home with Animus	18	11
5	Negative Animus	20	8
6	Positive Father	12	12
7	Negative Father	8	8
8	Idealized Father	8	2
9	Father's Anima	15	8
10	Love of Learning	17	13
11	Aggression	20	9
12	Death	11	2
13	Caged	20	13
14	Religion	11	10
15	Sexuality	17	9
16	Food	20	0
17	Lack of Body Contact as Child	12	7
18	Loss of Body Image	17	5
19	Loss of Feminine Identity	17	8
20	Basic Fear of Life	19	5
21	Fear of Rejection	19	10
22	Love of Nature	19	18
23	Fantasy Preferred to Reality	18	7
24	Longing for Childhood Paradise	15	4
25	Fear of Responsibility	4	4
26	Began Mother's Role as Child	12	4
27	Martyr	17	4
28	Rebel	17	12
29	Tomboy	9	9
30	Unwanted Child or Girl	3	4
31	Perfectionist	17	8
32	Outstanding Creativity	17	8
33	Above-average Intelligence	16	11
34	Hypersensitivity	19	14

Table 1. Complexes and personality traits of obese and controls.

ROW	HISTORY, EATING PATTERNS, ETC.	Column 1 Obese (of 20)	Column 2 Controls (of 20)
1	Fat as a Child	10	0
2	Fat at Puberty	17	2
3	Mother Fat	12	1
4	Father Fat	2	2
5	Parental Discord (Fear in home)	16	8
6	Lack of Money in Home (Fear of hunger)	10	4
7	Fear of Giving—Greed	9	4
8	Aloneness (Cut off from peer group—boys)	15	9
9	Aloneness (Cut off from peer group—girls)	14	7
10	Eating for Control	18	0
11	Eating in Depression	20	2
12	Eating in Repressed Anger	20	0
13	Eating in Anxiety	20	0
14	Eating for Illicit Satisfaction	8	0
15	Eating Replacing Sexuality	19	1
16	Food as Reward to Body	10	19
17	Food as Punishment	13	0
18	Withholding Food as Reward to Body	19	1
19	Withholding Food as Punishment to Body	1	0
20	Anger at Self	18	1
21	Anger at Fate	16	1
22	Guilt over Failure with Body	18	0
23	Overweight as Protection against Men	7	0
24	Overweight as Protection against own Animal	3	0
25	Gain Weight on 1000 Calories a Day	13	0
26	Diagnosed Edema	3	0
27	Body does not Properly Utilize Food	10	0
28	Menstrual Problems	4	1
29	Female Organ Operations	6	1
30	Chronic Constipation	11	4
31	Clothes	0	3
32	Alcohol	0	2
33	Smoking	0	3
34	Exercise and Garden	0	12

Table 2. History, eating patterns, etc., of obese and controls.

tions with food. The resultant anxiety often led to an early pattern of overeating coupled with an exaggerated dependence on self-control. This pattern can be so engrained that it may become a serious handicap when adjustment to later relationships is required.

In analysis, for example, if the transference is positive, the woman may have the confidence to relax her rigid dietary regime. She may allow herself to enjoy food, and more important, she may allow herself spontaneous response in relationship to others. If, however, the transference is or becomes negative, she will probably be filled with overwhelming anxiety which will force her to revert to the former control, and with it to the compulsive binges. So long as she adheres consciously to a strict diet, she is probably relating to the analyst and everyone around her on the same superficial level. There is then no possibility for the deeper instinctual levels which should be involved in the transference to constellate, and thus no hope for healing.

The voice of the negative animus thunders: "Thou shalt not, Thou shalt not, Thou shalt not." Imprisoned by that negativity, a child very early begins to live in terms of defence mechanisms and develops a protective shell which may seem to be a strong ego. This is a reactive pattern, however, which leaves the real person unconscious in her cage, unaware of her own need. Thus the fat girl often looks older than her years as a child, and younger than her years as an adult. Her secondhand feelings are not rooted in her own reality and therefore her unknown inner child lies buried in her adult body. While her own child starves, she feeds her animus—his fury, greed, ugliness, and jealousy—and is obliged to function without the positive bridge to her own unconscious.

Complexes and Personality Traits

1. Food

A careful examination of the data reveals at once the tyrannizing power of the food complex (Table 1, row 16). Food becomes the focus for *depression* (Table 2, row 11), for *repressed anger* (Table 2, row 12), for *anxiety* (Table 2, row 13), and for *repressed sexuality* (Table 2, row 15). It becomes a means of attempting to control one's fate, of expressing defiance of another's control (Table 2, row 10), defiance of the law and social customs (Table 1, row 28; Table 2, row 14), or even defying nature and God (Table 2, row 21).

Eight of the obese women admitted rejecting food at unhappy mealtimes with their families, preferring "barbaric snacks" out of the refrigerator; several took delight in stealing candy from supermarkets. "Honey, sweetheart, sugar" are all terms of endearment; from the cradle to the grave we look to the one we love for "food." The need for love is thus easily confused with the need for food. Since love is so much a part of life, tasting food is tasting life, but conversely, avoiding food may be avoiding life. The system of punishment and reward in relation to feeding the obese body becomes a moral issue. When they feel rejected by others, they tend to compensate their loss by eating (Table 2, row 16); when they are angry with themselves, they punish their bodies by eating (Table 2, row 17); when they are happy, they reward their bodies by not eating (Table 2, row 18). Only one obese woman suggested that self-imposed starvation was punishment to her body (Table 2, row 19). In short, food becomes the scapegoat for every emotion, and forms the nucleus around which the personality revolves.

The obsessive power of this complex must be kept in mind in order to understand the intensity of the emotions behind the other complexes. Obese women tend to shy away from the topic of food or to understate their emotions in relation to it. Only when they express their overwhelming sense of futility, and describe their suicidal tendencies, is the full impact of their powerlessness in the face of the obsession revealed. Their resultant fear and rage permeate all the other complexes.

COMMENTS ON FOOD (Table 1, row 16)

I feel noble when I diet. I feel it's good to deny myself.

I'm fed up with thinking about food. There must be a better way to live. For twenty-five years I've been running on that wheel like a gerbil in a cage. It's not human.

If I am happy or if I fall in love, I lose weight.

In order to cope with problems, I forget my 900 calories. When a problem arises, I am perverse.

I always lose weight when I am acting or writing. I always feel great when I am creating. I never feel weak despite the lack of food.

I operate at extremes—all control or no control. It's known as the yo-yo syndrome.

I think the concept of analgesic is right. Food is a painkiller. When life is unendurable, food is the best way to forget. It's good for avoidance, too. When I can't bring myself to do something, I nibble while I make my decision.

I eat to please others. eating is always part of a visit. Someone is giving me her love in the food. I try hard to please others.

When I binge, I feel like a moral slob.

There was a heavy-burdened atmosphere in our house. Control was rigid. Food was a comfort. It was joy. It was bribery and hospitality. My response to my own kids became food. If they were smoking pot, I would ask them if they wouldn't like something to eat.

Sometimes when I am watching others eating and I am not, I feel morally free. I don't have to eat. They do. Other times I feel morally inferior because I am tyrannized by weight. They do not have to worry about such a stupid thing. They are free. I am not.

I was never thin, not even during the war on a starvation diet. I can't lose weight on 400 calories a day. The doctor decided my war experience made it possible for my body to survive on what was put into it.

I love to bake but I don't like to be tempted to eat. It's like coming to orgasm and cutting myself off purposely. I can't wait to get old to get really fat.

Weight in me has something to do with hypertension. I gain weight when I'm tense no matter what I eat.

2. Mother

Jung, writing of the growing fear which besets the person who shrinks from adapting to reality, writes as follows:

> The fear of life is not just an imaginary bogey, but a very real panic, which seems disproportionate only because its real source is unconscious and therefore projected: the young, growing part of the personality, if prevented from living or kept in check, generates fear and changes into fear. The fear seems to come from the mother, but actually it is the deadly fear of the instinctive, unconscious, inner man who is cut off from life by the continual shrinking back from reality. If the mother is felt as the obstacle, she then becomes the vengeful pursuer. Naturally it is not the real mother, although she too may seriously injure her child by the morbid tenderness with which she pursues it into adult life, thus prolonging the infantile attitude beyond the proper time. It is rather the mother-imago that has turned into a lamia. The mother-imago, however, represents the unconscious, and it is as much a vital necessity for the unconscious to be joined to the conscious as it is for the latter not to lose contact with the unconscious.[17]

The women in this experiment were not pursued into adult life by the "morbid tenderness" of the mother, but rather by the clinging dependence of an adoring father or by their own desire for such a father-husband. However, "the young growing part of the personality" was in most cases rigidly disciplined by the animus of the mother, and the mother's "deadly fear of the instinctive, unconscious" inner woman.

The sins of the mother are visited from generation to generation, and the progressive loss of the feminine in our culture may be one of the chief causes of the escalating numbers of young women who reject their own bodies and hide behind their self-created Athena's *aegis*. Some are sensitive enough to recognize the parody of femininity that they are expected to emulate, and simply refuse to make that *rite de passage*. Whatever the reasons, the feminine libido is blocked, the feminine goddess is outraged and sends her ultimatum to the ego through the bloated body. Only by establishing communication with that unconscious force can the body ultimately be healed and the feminine spirit released.

COMMENTS ON MOTHER (Table 1, rows 1-4)

Mother always said, "That's not what you think." I overreacted to her rigid upbringing.

My mother took away my father's masculine pride. She reinforced his sense of failure. She worked hard to show us how ragged she had become. "You don't care about your mother," she would say.

I felt I was a nuisance to her. All the money I spent on her in my later years was to relieve the sense of guilt.

She was religiously clean—prissy—wore white gloves—cut off from life. My feelings towards my mother were very mingled. She lived through my academic prizes. "Any slut can have a baby," was her attitude.

When my brother was born, my mother's feelings turned to hatred for me. I adopt my mother's attitude—her horrid superiority. I hate myself for it. My dad was a little kid from the country.

Our house, it seems to me, is a natural force against natural rhythms—fat guinea pigs, fat cats, fat birds, fat kids, fat mother.

There are no associations with the word "love" in my head. No people, no objects that I can associate with the word. I was never loved—never. I was never cuddled by my parents. My mother tried to abort me before I was born. It didn't work. Here I am—a big balloon.

I would like to do something, but I am afraid. I am a little girl inside. At forty-two, I still need mother's approval for everything I do.

Mother never held me as a kid. She hated diapers and the fact that no matter what she gave I vomited it all back at her. From the beginning I felt rejected because of my body functions. I knew from the start that I was unloved because of my excretions. Now I am always constipated.

Mother never allowed me to do anything. I can't even ride a bicycle. I have no concept of anything creative. She was always showing off her breasts. Still is. Her father wanted a son. Tried to make her into a man. She is totally negative. No friends, no interests. I dread being like her, and I know I am.

In all sexual matters, Mother was a demon. I think she was possessed. I think she had been through such rejection by her puritan mother that she never recovered.

Mother got the idea that I was going to be fat. (She had been fat as a girl.) I became obsessed by the idea; by eleven I was fat. Mother prayed for miracles—that when I was fifteen I would be thin. I was a great chocolate cake baker. I believe that is a primary role of women—nourisher. I love people in the kitchen. I love children. I would love to marry and have children, instead of all these goddam books.

COMMENTS ON THE BASIC FEAR OF LIFE (Table 1, row 20)

Mother's sagas of our births, blow by blow, did nothing to encourage me to have children. I yearned for children once, but I feared they would be disillusioned by life as I am. I was terrified for them.

I want no children. If I make a work of art of my own life, that's OK. I will salvage something from the garbage.

I have no children. I missed life in the most important areas.

When I am afraid, I am cold. I am cold most of the time.

I was terrified at home and at school. Constantly terrified. I can cover my terror now.

I never lived. If only I could die and try again. I'm tired of trying now. I grieve for my unlived life.

I am still disturbed because I never wanted what other women take for granted—a home, children, husband.

All I have done all my life is to trip myself and fall.

I fear counting on anything giving me joy. It always explodes in my face. My philosophy is: Expect nothing, and you'll seldom be disappointed.

I always felt I wasn't smart enough to deal with any unknown situation.

It always comes back to the same thing. I can't find any meaning in life. I look from behind my bars, and wonder why other people seem so happy.

COMMENTS ON FEAR OF REJECTION (Table 1, row 21)

I am selfish, but I hate to be thought selfish. I throw up a smokescreen of politeness in order to be liked. If I told people what I think, I would destroy them.

I feel unlovable because of my body. I am full of self-rejection and feel unworthy to be loved.

I cannot look at myself in the mirror. I feel everyone hates me. I hate myself. I have no self-respect.

With adults, I shake. I am afraid. I stay with young people.

I am always fearful of men. I fear rejection from both men and women.

I don't know what I want to be in order to be acceptable to myself.

I come across to myself as a snivelling coward—fear talking to people, fear situations. "You're always going to be a dolt," I say to myself. "Always a crumb. Nobody will ever love you. Fat, ugly dolt."

3. Loss of Body Image, Sexuality, and Loss of Feminine Identity

The way in which we perceive our bodies is "a plastic concept which is built from all sensory and psychic experiences and is constantly integrated with the central nervous system."[18] In the obese woman the body image is distorted. The following comments suggest that the body image in some way precedes and determines the body structure. How the psychic sphere is reflected in her body is a question which the obese woman must face. The child absorbs the attitudes of others towards her body. If it does not conform to the socially acceptable image, she finds herself under enormous pressure. Her body size may be the result of disturbances, not only in hunger awareness but other bodily sensations as well. She must try to understand how her relationship to her body is mirroring the attitudes of significant people in her experience and, even more crucial, her attitude towards her own life. Through dreams and active imagination, she may accept the ownership of her own body, and thus her own reality.

COMMENTS ON LOSS OF BODY IMAGE (Table 1, row 18)

I have a good relationship to my body, but I don't like being tied to a dying animal.

I know I look like a pyramid turned upside down, but I can't help it.

I have no idea where I begin or where I end. I keep touching my body to try to figure out where my boundaries are.

The body is nothing. I know if I died tomorrow, my spirit would go on.

I'm in an empty prison.

I may have been cuddled by my parents, but there was certainly no naked playing around.

Last night I danced for the first time. I wasn't fighting this damned body. I was the dance.

Sometimes I think I cannot drag this load through life any farther. Just living seems a terrible load.

I love to buy clothes, but I never think of them on my body.

Heaviness is a protection. Men won't look at me. I hide behind it.

When I look in a mirror, I see myself the way I want to look.

I am repulsed by my body. My fat, I loathe it. I loathe myself because I am a failure. It's my own fault.

I hate being fat, but I haven't the moral fibre to change it. I don't have faith at fifty-one to believe I can diet again.

Sure I feel self-pity sometimes. I have to live in this body. Other people should be able to accept it for a few hours. I think others experience me as obscene.

Because my body has never been normal, I've had to develop psychic empathy with others; it's the only way I have to relate.

I have a terrible fear of disintegrating. Sometimes I feel I would fall into pieces if I didn't have my girdle to hold me together. It's a cage—physically and psychically—but I can't function without it.

Inside me, beneath my layers of fat, lives a slender, desirable, beautiful woman waiting to be born.

I like to talk to people on the telephone or in the dark. Then I can relax and be myself. I know they aren't put off by my ugliness.

It's not all bad being fat. Other people can't push me around. I feel real when I'm fat. I don't feel real when I'm thin.

I feel myself a human being in a fat shell.

I feel like an ant living in a glass environment.

When I'm fat, I'm not good friends with my body. When I'm thin I am. When I can talk to it, I'm nine-tenths out of the depression.

I'm apprehensive about losing weight. I'm so used to being fat. Losing weight isn't going to make life so great.

My car is more important to me than my body, more a part of me. When I think of myself, I think of my mind. When my car was struck, I was hurt emotionally. I cried. I can't stand pain.

COMMENTS ON SEXUALITY AND LOSS OF FEMININE IDENTITY
(Table 1, rows 15 and 19)

I'm really up in the air about my own sexuality. It takes real output, and I'm afraid of being rejected.

My size protects me and prevents me from loving men. I feel unworthy.

I knew I would never become pregnant.

I've been in mourning ever since my lover died. My real weight problem became impossible then. I'm just not motivated. Deep down I cannot face another failure, and so I don't try.

My body never stood between me and any man I wanted. If men don't like my fat body, tough bananas.

I never use contraceptives, never have. I know I will never conceive. I don't think of myself as a woman. I'm just me, whatever that is.

Anything below the waist terrifies me. It's all dirty.

Mother just gave me books to read and told me sex was a terribly messy business. When I began to have affairs, she pretended to hate them, but all she talked about to other women was my boyfriends. I was living out her desires.

I was terrified to become pregnant, because that would be an admission to the world that my husband and I were having sex. But I felt I had to have a son, because by giving my parents a grandson, I could justify my existence. They never accepted my being a girl.

My mother always tried to protect me from the danger of men. She never decked me out in pink and chiffon. I wear army shirts. . . . Sex in our marriage is an animal thing. I feel like a spittoon. . . . Father was imposing in his size. He never had to assert himself with others. He was a Rock of Gibraltar. He was big and generous in every way. Unconsciously I accept being fat. I am like him and I am glad I am like him.

I knew no man would ever love me.

I hate being a woman, hate taking second place. "Woman" is a put-down word, referring to unchaste Greek goddesses, sirens, and designing witches.

4. Father

Twelve women in each group had good relationships with their fathers ("positive" father, Table 1, row 6). Eight in each group had bad relationships with their fathers ("negative" father, Table 1, row 7). However, eight of the obese had idealized their negative father, by which I mean that their father was absent through business, alcoholism, divorce, or death, and therefore their imaginations had focussed on the perfect love to replace him. Only two of the controls had done so.

An important difference lies in the personality of the father and the dynamics between father, mother, and daughter. Among the controls, the positive father tended to be an authority figure, the man who went out into the world and helped the girl to relate to outside reality. Among the obese, the positive father was experienced as a saintly, idealistic, gentle puer, who related chiefly to his own inner world.

Where there was discord between the parents, the mother-anima of the father was frequently projected onto the daughter, who haplessly accepted it ("I look exactly like my father's mother. I am proud of that, and so is he "). This situation was compounded where the girl experienced her mother as negative. Among the controls, this anima tended towards athletic goals, whereas among the obese she sought spiritual and scholarly achievement, sometimes with sexual overtones. The emotional intensity of these father-daughter relationships cannot be measured. All that can be said is that the obese women tended to speak of their fathers—dead or alive—with immediacy and passion, suggesting that that specific relationship was not yet resolved. The controls, on the other hand, were putting their energy into the daily tension between themselves and men of their own age. The "ghostly lover" seemed to hover more darkly in the psyches of the obese than in those of the controls.

COMMENTS ON FATHER (Table 1, rows 6-8)

I never knew a man who was so kind; my father was a saintly man—so shy, so gentle.

My father made me too trusting of men. I expected too much. I tried to flow with it, but I always got hurt.

I am like my father's sister—intellectual, mannish.

I adored my father, but I realize now he valued me for my intellectual brilliance.

As a tiny child I was terrified of Father. I was afraid of doing wrong and having him reject me. I knew he didn't love me if I did anything to upset him. He was a protector; so long as he was there I was safe.

I tried to please Father as a child. Now I'm expected to please my husband. He's happy so long as I go around sleepwalking. He thinks I'm myself when I never speak back to him or cause him any trouble.

I am closer to my dad. I like to think of myself as his girl. I have his sensitivity. I'd rather be closer to him than my mom. At ten, I swore I'd never be like her. Everything she says is sarcastic. Sometimes I hear myself talking like her. I hate that.

I was supposed to have been a boy. It's a man's world. I absolutely wish I had been born a man. My qualities as a man would have been recognized. In a woman, they are a limitation. My father's qualities are my strong points.

COMMENTS ON LOVE OF LEARNING (Table 1, row 10)

I treasure books. I had free access to my father's library.

Dad started reading with me when I was three. I used to wait to get out of school to run home to read with him.

My love of poetry, my literary tradition, I associate with my father.

In my trapped world, books are my only chance of survival. My father taught me to love the Bible. I read it now because I love it.

COMMENTS ON FATHER'S ANIMA (Table 1, row 9)

I was Dad's girl.

Father says, "If only you were beautiful. If only you would do something about your weight and hair." I stuff myself when I am with my father. He gives me no love at all, although he is fiercely attracted to me sexually. He is endlessly greedy. He sucks at me. I couldn't do enough for him. Mend, clean—everything. Nothing is enough. Even if I went to bed with him, someone could do it better. He wants no one else in his house. He harps at me about how beautiful other girls are. Then I shovel food into my mouth.

Daddy's little anima has to be this woman he wants her to be—a mother with four sons, Matthew, Mark, Luke and John. I would like to raise a little girl—the child in me that never got born.

Overweight protected me from my father's sexuality. As a teenager I feared if I ever got going in sex, I'd be a wild animal.

My father always made fun of my boyfriends. He said we would love them to death. They always left.

My puberty period really turned my father on. Really he should be shot.

In my mind my father was a perfect, brilliant, sensitive, spiritual man. And he loved me—God, how he loved me. But what I had to pay was everything.

My father gave me all the money I needed and sucked my life blood in return. I thought he was the most wonderful father until I realized he had taken away even my intellectual freedom.

Father wanted me to stay in the Paradise he had created for me—for us. He was afraid of life and planned that we should stay together so long as he lived.

5. Religion

Behind the positive father complex or the unconscious identification with the positive father lies the "loving God" imago. In worshipping Him, the girl learns to esteem courage, rational control, and spiritual goals above everything else. Perfection is demanded of her, and she demands perfection of others. The perfect scheme does not countenance weakness, stupidity, fear or gluttony. When she cannot discipline her own hunger, or when her body refuses to give up the weight, she experiences herself as powerless and the problem takes on a suprapersonal dimension.

In the early stages of the struggle, she tends to feel personal guilt and a loss of self-respect, but harbours a certain defiant hope. Gradually, her sense of justice questions a God whom she had tried so hard to please, but who nevertheless punishes her in her most vulnerable spot. Like Job, she believes herself to be righteous beyond the call of duty and therefore her situation is incomprehensible to her. Progressively—partly through feelings of deprivation, and partly through physical and psychic fatigue—she slips into silent despair. She may talk of the will of God with child-like faith, but viciously mock her personal weakness in being unable to control her own life.

Of the women involved in this study, only those in analysis could deal with "evil" except as an abstract word; for the others, evil was projected and they experienced themselves as victims of a dark Fate, always in relation to their weight. Essentially, they were unaware of their own shadows which had taken somatic form in their rejected bodies.

COMMENTS ON RELIGION (Table 1, row 14)

Before I could turn to God as my father; now I see Him as the devil too.

I cannot be conventionally religious. I almost pass out at communion. But I do believe in God. I used to think of Him as a kind, loving father. Now I am all confused. How could a loving God do this to me? There's no justice in this.

I dreamed that Christ would be born out of my fat thighs.

I am chased by the Hound of Heaven. When I can't run fast enough, I eat.

I used to believe that people who believed in God were weak. They couldn't control their own lives. I had to be totally broken to learn humility. In order to accept the gift of humility, you have to have strength.

I feel terrible guilt. I don't know why. I feel I have to do everything my husband wants to do or I am guilty. I think I am selfish wanting things for myself. Then I can't do anything for myself.

I've accepted my pain and my forgiveness, but I fear Satan may attack me through my children.

I yearn to do the right thing, or what people think is the right thing. I have always overwhelming self-doubt about what "right" is.

I avoid the evil of my flabby arms. I slipped into sloth.

I think it is evil that I don't have enough sense to save my life—just go on eating. The mountain is here and Mohammed hasn't been able to move it.

COMMENTS ON ANGER AT FATE (Table 2, rows 20 and 21)

I am angry at Fate over my body. I try not to question too much. Try to make the best of things. I used to fantasize, but not now.

"Why can Someone not help me?" I ask. I feel downed. But I've learned to live on automatic pilot. When I go down, I know how to come up. I have a party, prepare food, etc. Depression makes me work; it never keeps me from doing things.

I find it hard to love a God who made me this way. I'd rather be crippled. At least people wouldn't think me just a fat slob. Sometimes I think I can't go any further but I'm afraid to commit suicide.

I feel God has put this on me. I was brought up to believe that Jesus Christ was walking beside me. I've been forced to look at His darkness. . . . If it were right with God, it would be right with my body. If I am not in proper relationship to God I am not in proper relationship to myself. If I haven't got a good relationship to a man, I can't have a good relationship to God. When I get no nourishment spiritually from man or God, I have to eat. I gobble food.

COMMENTS ON PERFECTION (Table 1, row 31)

I am my Dad's masterpiece. This masterpiece has to justify its existence.

I try to push beyond my endurance. I was a perfectionist twenty years ago. I like to think I have matured. Some things can be perfect; others can't.

My house is like a stage setting. I love to organize things over and over again. I love to believe it looks cosy but I am not connected to it. I want the people who come in to be perfect—my husband especially. If they show me their imperfections, I hate them. I'll torture myself for years if I make a mistake.

Perfection. Perfection. That was all I longed for. Still have to watch myself. I still feel I have to justify my existence because I am bright.

Do everything as perfectly as possible. That's my motto. Wring the best out of every day with an ocean of ambition and a puddle of achievement. I am an extremist. If I put my name to it, I want it to be well done.

I despise stupidity in myself and others. I am a perfectionist.

Perfection is achieved not when there is nothing left to add, but when there is nothing left to take away. That's why I loathe a fat body.

I knew I was important, but that depended on my performance. I was a production, a masterpiece. Therefore, I could not fail.

6. Fantasy Preferred to Reality

In the relationship where the father feared reality, his daughter was likewise infected and sought to escape with him into a fantasy world. Eighteen of the obese preferred fantasy to reality, and fifteen yearned for a paradise which they had known or dreamed of with their fathers. The controls tended to be more realistic. Several in both groups expressed doubt concerning their fathers' love for them as individuals. Looking back they saw themselves as dolls being manipulated to please their fathers' ideals. Where circumstances forced the girl into taking on the maternal role as a child, the longing for the childhood she never had was still evident (Table 1, row 26).

COMMENTS ON FANTASY PREFERRED TO REALITY (Table 1, row 23)

I eat instead of dealing with my problems. I do not deal with life.

I cannot get enough sleep. I don't see myself in my dreams. Not important to me in my sleep whether I'm fat or thin.

I love to dream. I get away from the obsession.

Conflict—that's my life. Conflict between what I am and what I dream I am.

COMMENTS ON LONGING FOR CHILDHOOD PARADISE (Table 1, row 24)

I wish I could have remained at seven. I was happy. I had no responsibility.

I was "Little Miss Sunshine" as a child. My heart didn't start crying until I went to school.

I feel I am an innocent, childlike creature hiding somewhere. I am scared to death of being incapable in this world.

I feel I lost out on my childhood. Now I'd like to stretch out my childhood over my whole life.

I was forced into adulthood at ten. I used to resent having lost my childhood and adolescence; I carried the whole fuckin' family.

I took on adult responsibility at five. My mother was ill and I felt responsible for the younger children. I don't know any role but mother. Now I don't fear responsibility, but I don't want it.

I never had a childhood. All my life I've been living out a shadow thing for my mother. Her father was Jesus Christ even though He used to kick her. Mother never accepted me as I am. She projected her creativity onto me. I carried her bloody load from the beginning.

7. Aggression

Helpless rage is rarely expressed by obese women. For the most part, they were self-effacing, compliant little girls whose chief joy in life was to please Daddy. Mother disciplined their spontaneous outbursts of anger, joy, or tears, and they unconsciously turned their aggression against themselves. Their unexpressed feelings live in the cage of their compulsive drives waiting to burst out. Generally, they realize that the energy is blocked in the body, but they are powerless to release it. One of their responsibilities is to recognize the memories that are stored in the body from infancy. All their fears of rejection and annihilation are caged in their fat bodies along with the compensating anger and desire for power. Where the woman has been fat from childhood, she has probably experienced herself as a social

outcast from the beginning and her ego development may be seriously impaired.

Esther Harding, referring to the ego complex preceding the formation of a conscious ego, writes:

> Where the ego is inadequately developed in modern adults and is not
> made conscious, we find that the ego complex remains in the uncon-
> scious and functions from there. In consciousness an individual repre-
> senting this level of development may be conspicuously lacking in
> that concentration and centredness which is characteristic of the per-
> son with more conscious ego development; yet egotism and will to
> power, of which the unevolved person is unaware, may function none-
> theless and produce their inevitable effects on all with whom he comes
> in contact. . . . [Where] egotism and self-will are in the unconscious . . .
> they manifest themselves in somatic, that is, in pre-psychological form. . . .
> When the ego comes to consciousness and the individual becomes
> aware of himself as I, the reaction to difficulties or obstructions will
> no longer appear in physical form as symptoms but will be recognized
> in consciousness as emotions. That is to say, the reaction will be a
> psychological one. . . . The emergence of the ego from the unconscious
> brings with it a new problem, the problem of the will to power.[19]

If a woman is to be freed of neurotic symptoms she must renounce
unconscious methods of getting her own way, and face life more
directly, thus gaining real power over both herself and her environment.

If in later life she has mastered her hunger drive by ego control,
she may assume that she can control her fate herself. But that ego
may in fact be very weak, because it has been built by cutting herself off from the mainstream of life through severe dieting. It is
built on negative rather than positive need. In a real life crisis, such
an ego may fail to operate because she does not know consciously
what her own needs are. Again the unconscious will inundate her.
She will cry out against Fate; her bloated body may become an expression of her powerless ego and her fear of annihilation. At the
same time, however, the body is protecting itself against death in its
rebellion against her will-power. The martyr-rebel ambivalence (Table
1, rows 27 and 28) lies in this conflict. Part of her is forced to accept
what she believes is her destiny; part of her rebels against "false
justice." An ego which sets itself up against Fate is attempting to
usurp the power of the Self; it swings from light to dark, from inflation to depression. Only when her ego is firmly rooted in her own
feminine feeling can a woman be released from her compulsive behaviour.

COMMENTS ON AGGRESSION (Table 1, row 11)

A caged tiger is terrible to see. All that power picking at its own lice.

Anger is never dealt with in our family. It is destructive because it is underground. I ignore my anger, or don't feel it, then suddenly "BANG."

Binge eating is punishing myself. It is a totally destructive act, always followed by depression.

I have a fierce temper. I cannot abide disorder.

I can be vicious. Fury blinds me, but I never lash out. I often wake up yelling.

When I am furious with Dick, I tear open the fridge door, and grab anything I can find and wolf it down.

I am capable of murder. I used to lie on the floor and bang my head. Takes a lot to arouse me, but once angry, I frighten people.

I rarely fight—no need to. I am proud not to fight. But then I always turn against myself and eat. Sometimes I take a knife to myself. Nothing can stop me. I never feel it is wrong. Afterwards I have a strong sense of relief. I've finished something. I have to bring things to a crisis in order to remedy the situation. I have no desire to end my life. I just want to hurt myself. The physical motion brings to consciousness the fact that I need help.

I hate the feeling of anger because it is self-directed. My anger always contains the fear of truth.

As a child I never won. I know I never will.

I was held back at every point in a very restricted environment. I guess I want revenge.

COMMENTS ON FEELING CAGED (Table 1, row 13)

My first painting for my analyst came right from my gut—a black owl with huge vacant eyes weeping drops of scarlet blood.

When I am happy, all the controls are off. I have to be careful because I don't think as I should. I drive too fast. I don't obey the law. Life is free. I am free. I eat whatever I like in that released freedom. I almost fear freedom, for fear of what might happen. Would I eat and gain pounds? Or would the freedom burn the calories? Would the blocked energy be burned? Would I, in fact, have lost weight?

Life is a box closing in ever faster and faster. The harder I struggle, the more the box closes in.

There is a creative self that isn't getting release. My husband doesn't like me to shine. I can't speak as I feel.

There is no freedom. I am trapped. I don't ask to eat sweets. I only want to eat a normal meal. That's where the resentment comes in, and the guilt.

This weight thing is "the mark of the beast." If I were in harmony with the infinite, I don't think I would have this problem. It has always been a terrible torment, a constant tyranny. If I were tuned properly, if the trammels were off, I wouldn't have this problem.

My recurrent fantasy is to run into a field and swing around with my arms in the air, shouting my lungs out as if I had just been let out of a cage, just experienced the first freedom I have ever known.

I often feel like a duck with its wings pinned against its sides inside an oven.

I want freedom. I can't be in one place too long without feeling restless. My car is a box but it is going somewhere. I'm tired of life's problems so I have a fear of programmes of self-improvement. The first problem and I would collapse so I haven't the courage to start.

There's no way out. I've tried every diet. I've taken amphetamines till I couldn't stop shaking. I joined Weight Watchers and Vic Tanny's. I've been to homeopaths and acupuncture specialists. At forty-six, I've gained and lost over 1000 pounds and I'm still fat.

COMMENTS ON POWER (not in table)

I'd probably be the strong one in a marriage. I would not like that. I wouldn't like it at all—but it would probably be that way. Mother is the strong one in our family. My father resents strong women, but he would fall apart without her.

I resent taking orders especially from men.

I love my car. I always do the driving.

If I thought I didn't have life under my control, I would be really upset. Don't like the idea of Fate controlling. Don't think I could go on if I didn't think I had control.

I've always been the strong woman. The only strong man I've ever known was the one I didn't marry.

I would like a man to take care of me; I've accepted the fact that it won't happen. All the men in my life I've taken care of.

I don't want to have power, because I don't want the responsibility. I just can't be bothered. It would be good to have a feeling of control; it would guarantee me a freedom of choice.

I am a tyrant. I like to control life. I was born to be strong. No one wants a lady on a couch.

COMMENTS ON THE REBEL (Table 1, row 28)

My sense of justice has nothing to do with conventional law.

Something in me refuses to starve just to be like other people.

I am very ordered and controlled, and then something snaps in my head and I do what I want to do.

I like my little schemes. Food is important for illicit satisfaction. The criminal element is only marginally controlled.

The life I live is so abnormal any normal reaction would be abnormal.

I have no idea what a "normal" life is, I hate fitting into a mould. I've always been different from my peer group.

COMMENTS ON THE MARTYR (Table 1, row 27)

I go further than most people in allowing their needs to dictate my actions.

I am a built-in martyr.

I don't think it's important to know who I am. I am utilizing my talents being of service to others. Helping others—that is what is important. I don't love myself. I don't agree with Fromm that you have to love yourself in order to love others. I've accepted conditions in my life now. I should not resent what I was born with.

I don't want pity. I feel sorry for myself, but then it's my own fault.

My lover is a sweet, lovable puppydog. I figure this is yet another that I am going to look after.

I always have to think about the other person. I've spent my whole life being dishonest. Since childhood, I've covered up for my drunken grandfather and drunken father.

8. Death

The death complex, while voiced by only eleven obese volunteers, was implicit in their comments concerning their fear of life and their conscious and unconscious rage against themselves. The fear of drowning was repeatedly mentioned. While this may be interpreted as a fear of the unconscious, it also expresses a fear of unconsciously slipping into death. Unintentional suicide could take the form of a fatal illness. A sense of helplessness permeated their outlook, thus giving to death a magnetic attraction and repulsion. Statistically, however, the suicide rate is significantly lower in the obese, suggesting that as a defence reaction obesity may have a positive value.[20]   But this also means that when the real feelings surface through the withdrawal of food, then the danger of suicide increases. Despair may replace eating. Life may be rejected, consciously or unconsciously, through the rejection of food as in anorexia nervosa. While elaborate eating rituals may protect the young anorexic from her feelings, a despairing woman may silently decide to make her slow escape through self-starvation.

COMMENTS ON DEATH (Table 1, row 12)

I have a terrible fear of being taken over by another person. Sometimes it is a Darkness that overtakes me. That fear makes me hold back from Life, withhold what I could give.

I am haunted by fear. Maybe it's fear of the Evil Eye. I am afraid to express too much joy for fear it will be taken from me. I fear something may happen to my children.

Almost every morning I have to choose to live.

Sometimes I am compelled to dare Life to its very extremities. I have to face Death in order to know what Life is.

I will probably die of cancer. That will be God's curse upon me. Death is the end of suffering.

I wish for death many times. When a child can't have his sucker, he says he didn't want it in the first place.

Ever since I was seventeen, I've toyed with the idea of suicide. It's only will-power that keeps me going. Some day I'll give up.

Controls

I have emphasized the responses of the obese because this is essentially a study of eating disorders. The conflicts of the controls would in themselves make an interesting study of 20th-century women. Some general comparisons, however, are relevant here.

The one common factor in both groups was the love of nature as comforter and restorer (Table 1, row 22). Beyond that, the controls broke into two groups: those with a positive, and those with a negative mother. Fifteen of the controls, because they had positive mothers, loved life, loved being women, loved their own sexuality, and had an inner conviction of their own worth. They had no problem identifying with their own bodies.[21] They were able to express their emotions, notably anger, in spontaneous response to immediate

	Total	Age range	Mean overweight	Middle class income	Married no children	Married with children	Canadian or American	UK
Obese	20	19-64	ca.40 lbs.	20	12	7	18	2
Controls	20	18-54	0	20	16	16	15	5

	Number in analysis	Students	High school education	University Graduates	Careers	Career and Home
Obese	5	4	20	10	11	7
Controls	5	2	20	12	13	3

Table 3. Comparison of obese and control population data.

situations. They dealt with their problems in a straightforward feminine way, that is to say from some instinctual wisdom inherited from their mothers, which allowed them to "feel" what was right in a situation. Many of the obese had a positive relationship with their mothers (often to the point of identification), but where the mother was not in touch with her own femininity, the daughter inherited a negative mother complex.

The five controls with negative mothers formed an important subgroup because their problems, apart from food, tended to be more like those of the obese, especially in relation to the body, sexuality, feminine identity, and basic fear of life. Like the other controls, they spoke of enjoying good food as a part of life, but like the obese they had more difficulty in making a diet work. Most could eat over 1500 calories a day without gaining weight. Seven of the controls had problems with drinking or smoking.

Thirteen of the controls expressed the "caged" feeling but never in relation to their bodies. Usually it came from not feeling free to be themselves for fear of offending the men in their lives. This statement suggests that the cage or prison has something to do with living an artificial or provisional life, which is often the result of trying-to live out other people's projections instead of being oneself. Where the woman is unaware of her authentic being, she will try to fill her emptiness with some subtitute.

Thus, in the obese woman, we have the image of the body as a cage built of others' false projections while her own inner emptiness is filled with food; in the normal weight woman the cage is less tangible. In both cases, however, the key is in the hands of the negative animus, which may, paradoxically, be projected onto the beloved man.

One thing seemed clear. Where the mother was unquestionably in touch with her femininity, she had given to her daughter a love of being a woman and a basic faith in life. Such a woman need not come into analysis because she can grow through actual life situations. She develops *cum natura.* Where the mother is negative, the daughter is from the beginning hampered in making emotional adjustments and fails to take the natural steps towards feminine maturity. If she enters analysis, those *rites de passage* which she failed to make in reality, she may make symbolically. The natural physical processes and their images are worked through consciously in a psychological and spiritual dimension, *contra naturam.*

Only if the girl has been allowed to live her own life as a child, and has learned to value herself and her feelings, will she be able to cope with reality in a creative way. The heritage of the mother and the father's respect for the mother as a feminine being are crucial to this natural maturing.

Conclusions

In general, primary and secondary obesity must be differentiated and treated differently. The time and cause of onset of obesity are crucial in determining the manner of treatment.

Family Background of Obese Woman

1. Family probably oriented towards food for varying emotional needs.
2. Mother usually unconscious of her own femininity, out of touch with her own body and sexuality.
3. Mother tended to be domineering towards whole family, rejected the girl as an individual, and projected her own unlived life onto the child.
4. Mother probably considered the father weak and incompetent in his relationship to the world.
5. Daughter's experience of the masculine may have been through her mother's animus; therefore, a deep-seated fear of the "masculine" developed. All spontaneity in the home was rigidly disciplined, resulting in the child's lack of body awareness and loss of contact with her own emotional needs.
6. Mother's unconscious rejection of her own and her daughter's femininity resulted in feelings of rejection, which are stored as body memories and feelings of guilt and inadequacy.
7. Because the mother was not able to give love, she may have been overprotective and indulgent with food.
8. Daughter forced into maternal role too early, therefore rejects mature maternal role, prefers to remain a child.
9. Father tended to give the daughter the warmth and nourishment she needed. Tendency towards confusion in gender roles and generation boundaries results in intense bond between father and daughter.

10.   Father's disappointment in his wife resulted in anima projec-
      tion onto daughter. Essentially, however, he was unable to love
      her for herself. Unconsciously she felt this and denigrated her
      own self-worth. Later in life her deep-seated guilt and fear re-
      sult in the inability to make demands from her own feminine
      reality, thus inviting the rejection she fears.

11.   Daughter felt the hopes and dreams of both parents pinned on
      her. Tried so hard to fulfil these that she was and is unaware of
      her own innate potential.

Personality Problems of Obese Woman

1.   Tends to live life in terms of other people's needs and reactions.
     May compensate by becoming fiercely possessive. Danger of be-
     coming an automaton.

2.   Convinced of her own unworthiness, therefore hypersensitive
     to rejection. May be compensated by an inflated view of her
     own self-worth. The unconscious body mirrors this in its size.

3.   As an adult, still dependent on the mother or father, at the same
     time rebellious against them.

4.   Life a desperate search for her own identity, physically and
     psychically. Wants to feel she is in control of her own body and
     own life. Without this, a growing sense of despair develops.

5.   Fears social contact with her peer group, develops an overwhelm-
     ing sense of aloneness and loneliness.

6.   Weak ego leads to inability to cope with reality, and flights into
     fantasy with a princely father or his surrogate. Fantasies tend
     to be very inflated.

7.   Unaware of own shadow. Feels herself manipulated and victim-
     ized by evil forces from outside (e.g., parents, Devil, God), but
     blind to the personal reality of evil.

8.   "Passivity" terrifies her. No understanding of positive feminine
     energy. "To surrender" for her means giving up, cowardice,
     loss of control, annihilation. Cannot understand "losing one's
     life to find one's life," either sexually or spiritually. Resultant
     fear of sexuality, spontaneous feeling, and orgasm.

9.   Devoted to Apollinian order and discipline. Terrified of any-
     thing remotely smacking of the Dionysian, therefore prone to
     possession by it (e.g. midnight binges).

The Obese Woman and Her Body

1. Does not experience herself and her body as one. Body takes on the projection of the shadow and is experienced as evil. Sexuality therefore becomes evil. Femininity and sexuality are confused.

2. Unable to experience her own body size. Does not know physically or psychically where she begins or where she ends.

3. Cannot recognize her own bodily functions, therefore misunderstands signals from the body, especially "hunger."

4. Rigidity towards feelings results in physical rigidity and blocked energy.

5. Frustrations, aggressions, and inability to adjust to reality are expressed in craving for food.

6. Tension in the body for whatever reason relieved through eating.

7. Overeating and obesity may be defence against psychotic break.

8. Not eating and being slim considered synonymous with being good, courageous, morally strong, beautiful, capable, successful, feminine, and desirable. Losing weight would put all these fantasies to the test.

9. Obesity often an expression of defiance towards collective values, especially the cultural emphasis on thinness.

10. Fantasies of perfection lead to "all or nothing" attitudes which discourage moderate dieting.

11. Large body may give feeling of strength and stability, compensating lack of self-confidence and feelings of inadequacy.

While many of these conclusions could apply to other types of neurotic disturbances, the obese woman is driven by her preoccupation with weight and that factor must always be kept in mind.

In interpreting this data, I have kept two questions in mind: Why does one woman become fat, while another remains thin? What does the fat symbolize?

In answer to the first, the genetic and environmental influences are most important. A woman must very honestly look at her forebears and her own personal history and then try to act in harmony with nature. Statistically, 80% of overweight parents have overweight children, whereas only 10% will be overweight if the parents are not.[22]

Environmental influences exert themselves very quickly in infancy and the individual must discern whether what seems genetic is truly genetic, or whether her parents, too, were overfed as children. Fat people generally come from families who were quite oral in their orientation to life. Great value was set on the giving and receiving of food. It carried emotional overtones for every situation: parents who could not give love gave food; parents who had little money took pride in a good table; parents who valued cultural traditions conveyed these to their children through sumptuous feast-days; parents who repressed their own sexuality tended to compensate with food. The other pleasures which should have developed as the obese child matured never found the same value in her psyche. Once aware of how important food—or even fatness—is to her, she may be able to accept the increased anxiety when she deprives herself of sweet carbohydrates.

The answer to the second question, "What does fat symbolize?" is the substance of the rest of this book. Sufficient to say here that the fat body may be both a womb and a tomb. If she sees it as a tomb, the woman may be too ready to give up her search for her own life force which is buried alive within her. If she has the courage to look in the mirror and actually see her own dark side—without identifying with it—she may be able to see her fatness symbolically, and thus find the objectivity to suffer the pain of awareness. The fat has to be "put in the fire" in order to produce growth. She must face her own shadow in order to find the treasure; consciously relating to her body can give her the opportunity to relate to her own unconscious feminine feeling.

Instead of escaping into eating or animus activity, the obese woman must take up her own cross and carry it. This for her is accepting the opposites and enduring the pain until the resurrected body can be born. The woman with a negative mother and a positive father may be doubly unconscious. Her task is to release her own creative masculine spirit from the womb of the devouring mother, and at the same time to release her own feminine spirit from the tomb of her Jehovah father.

SOME FACTORS TO BE CONSIDERED BY THE THERAPIST OR ANALYST OF THE OBESE WOMAN

1. What are my conscious and unconscious feelings towards a fat woman?

2. Can I respect this woman as an individual and hear what she is saying without a "think-thin" bias?

3. Is she primarily obese? If so, can I help her to accept her size and live with it happily?

4. At what age did her preoccupation with food begin to hamper her emotional development?

5. Is the obesity a part of her lifetime pattern? Did it gradually develop? Is it a reaction to some traumatic event?

6. Can I imagine how it feels to live in a body which I do not experience as my own?

7. Can I help her to experience and understand the feelings locked in her body without imposing my own intellectual interpretation?

8. Will her physician cooperate with me?

9. Does she know how much she eats? Can she tell the truth about her eating habits?

10. Is she suffering from nutritional deficiencies? Are her moods related to sudden fluctuations in her eating patterns?

11. Is food for this woman an addiction representing an unmet symbolic need and/or an escape from reality?

12. Does she have vital needs which are being satisfied by food? Would dieting at this point create more serious psychological problems (e.g., danger of suicide)?

13. Are her expectations of being thin related to reality? Will losing weight solve or accentuate her psychological problems?

14. Is her self-discipline concerning food reflected in rigid control of her feelings? Is her quiet, composed manner and her "normal" attitude towards food hiding a break in the transference?

15. Can she distinguish between fantasy and reality? Can I distinguish between what is real and what is performance in her speech and actions? Can I keep my sense of humour?

16. Is there any danger of a psychotic episode if this woman (especially if young) loses weight?

CHAPTER II

THE BODY AND THE PSYCHE

. . . . we are not ourselves
When nature being oppressed commands the mind
To suffer with the body.

—*King Lear*

It is now generally accepted that psyche and body are one and indivisible. Therefore, a brief study of body metabolism is essential to a psychological understanding of the somatic problems of obesity. Research during the past thirty years has made it quite clear that energy balance in the body is not solely dependent on input of calories and expenditure of energy; medical journals contain countless reports on experiments introducing new factors, psychic and somatic, which must be considered.

Since I am neither a biochemist nor an endocrinologist, I am unqualified to discuss the intricate balance of hormones, enzymes, and biochemical pathways of energy in the body.[23] As an analyst, however, when working with an obese patient I am aware of her alienation from her body. It has become her enemy. She has followed a no-fat diet, a high-fat diet, a 1000-calorie-a-day diet—all to no avail. Her body swells and recedes according to its own whims and, for the most part, she has given up trying to understand it. Her physician, unless he is well read in modern research, believes that she is yet another "fatty" who hasn't the will-power to follow her diet, and he must devote his attention to those who genuinely need him.

From a physiological point of view, therefore, it is essential that an intelligent woman learn for herself the body mechanisms; her body has its individual nutritional needs and she may find renewed interest in experimenting with foods that she can or cannot metabo-

44

lize properly. Moreover, in my experience, many obese women are intuitives, whose inferior function is sensation. They become fascinated with their dream images and tend to ignore the body in which the shadow is embedded, a situation which will eventually lead to disease or "possession." This one-sided consciousness can be corrected by focusing attention on a creative approach to the body—a loving understanding of its unique mechanism. They may become increasingly fascinated with the details of caring for it, and thus bring it and its psychic problems into consciousness.

This encounter will inevitably bring about the conflict of opposites, which they must endure if they are to grow. From a psychological point of view, it is essential that an obese woman face her shadow problem as evidenced in her body. With this in mind, there are certain basic biological facts, so far as we know them today, which are of value in a therapeutic situation.

Body Metabolism

The body is a magnificently tuned machine, programmed to metabolize carbohydrate, protein, and fat.

Fuel from food or fat stores	+	Oxygen	=	Energy (heat produced for mental and physical activity)	+	Carbon dioxide and water (waste products)

The hypothalamus, an area of the brain just above and connected to the pituitary gland, coordinates the action of all the hormones in the body, including those which control appetite and the menstrual cycle. It receives the message "hunger" from the lowered level of glucose in the blood; this is coordinated with the increased contractions of the empty stomach, perceived by the higher centres of the brain and interpreted as hunger. The blood sugar range must be maintained because glucose is essential for energy to the brain; it cannot break down protein or fat. Glucose comes from carbohydrate and/or liver glycogen and is the most rapidly usable energy source for any cell. The blood sugar is normally maintained in the range of 80-120 mg%. If 100 grams of sugar in water are ingested, within minutes they are absorbed into the blood. Within half an hour, the pancreas receives the message to release insulin which forces the sugar to enter the cells in all parts of the body. After one to one-and-a-half hours, the blood sugar begins to fall and within three to four hours the curve goes down to normal.

The blood is maintained within a normal blood sugar range by a homeostatic mechanism known as hepatic glycogenolysis. In this process, when the blood sugar falls below the individual's normal range, the liver releases glucose from glycogen, the form in which carbohydrate is stored. When the glycogen stores are depleted, the liver then resorts to the synthesis of glucose from protein stores, a process known as gluconeogenesis, thus making sugar available to the blood. Fats likewise are broken down step by step for energy purposes. Whereas glucose is completely and efficiently metabolized, breaking down into water and carbon dioxide, fat is broken down less completely with many intermediate metabolites, i.e., fatty acids and ketones.

This is nature's basic process. Hunger is a physiological drive which must eventually be satisfied. However, the person suffering from an eating disorder tends to confuse "hunger" and "appetite" because, as is clear from the experimental material in Chapter I, food has acquired connotations far beyond bodily nourishment. When this confusion has continued over a period of years, certain physiological changes have taken place which make the hunger bell ring sooner than it does in normal appetite. Dr. Jay Tepperman, an acknowledged authority, distinguishes between the two in the following definition:

> Hunger is the awareness of the need to ingest food, and it may be accompanied by a complex set of phenomena, including hunger pangs, anticipatory salivation, increased food-searching behaviour, and others. In sum, hunger is a malaise, a disagreeable combination of sensations which, as it progresses, acquires frantic character. . . . Appetite is the desire to ingest food. Unlike hunger which occurs when the body's store of nutrients becomes depleted below a certain preset maintenance level, appetite may persist when hunger has been appeased. Appetite is strongly influenced by emotion, by the presence or absence of conditioning and distracting stimuli, and by discriminatory choices of various kinds. Satiety is the lack of desire to eat which occurs after the ingestion of food.[24]

When food is fulfilling emotional needs, satiety is either not recognized or ignored physiologically. The person who has become dependent on food as a soporific to ease anxiety, frustration, and emotional emptiness does not binge on protein and fat; she craves sweetness, and that sweetness she finds in carbohydrates. If the system is disturbed by long-term overconsumption of carbohydrates, or if the individual is genetically pre-disposed, insulin becomes less and less effective, until diabetes is the result. In that disease, the sugar goes into circulation, but instead of going into the cell, it remains unutilized because the insulin is ineffective; therefore, the blood sugar continues to rise and remains elevated. The correlation between diabetes and obesity is well know, and the obese individual frequently has a diabetic-like curve because her body requires more insulin.[25]

Hypoglycemia (too little sugar in the blood) may have organic causes, but functional hypoglycemia is usually caused by overreaction to carbohydrates. The overtaxed pancreas responds with too much insulin and the blood sugar drops too low. Fatigue and depression, always components in the obesity syndrome, have a biochemical as well as a psychic cause; they are symptoms of low blood sugar. Carbohydrate gives the temporary lift to energy and sagging spirit, but when the blood sugar level drops, many symptoms besides fatigue and depression may appear, such as irritability, dizziness, headache, faintness, and confusion.

Some Contemporary Views on Obesity

Most doctors are vehement in their condemnation of the modern diet, so overloaded with sugar and refined carbohydrates, because the natural body mechanism is not equipped to deal with these unnatural foods. Such a diet is no doubt partially responsible for the fact that obesity has become one of our culture's most important public health problems. It is a concomitant of many chronic diseases. According to Beeson and McDermott, 30% of American males and 40% of American females are twenty pounds or more overweight.[26]

Poorer nutritional value in modern food may be a factor. Calorie intake in our highly mechanized society need not be so great as it was for our pioneer grandfathers, but our protein and vitamin needs are the same. Instant foods may leave our bodies genuinely hungry for essential nutrients, and therefore they call for more calories in an attempt to fulfil their vitamin, mineral, and protein requirements.

Since most compulsive eating is uncontrollable wolfing of concentrated carbohydrates, and since a high protein and/or high fat diet is often successful when the 1000-calorie-a-day diet has failed, widespread interest has focused on diets that purport to change the body metabolism. Essentially, this means that when the liver no longer has available carbohydrate resources, it turns to gluconeogenesis, converting proteins, and working with the rest of the body, converting fat stores for energy.

Dr. Richard Mackarness, a psychiatrist who directs an obesity and food allergy clinic in Basingstoke, England, believes that obesity may be caused by an intolerance or hypersensitivity to too-concentrated a diet of refined carbohydrates.

> Fat is the *least* fattening of all foods because, in the absence of carbohydrates, it (and to a lesser extent protein) turns the bellows on the body fires in a fat person and enables him to mobilize his stored fat as well as helping him to burn up the food he eats more efficiently. On a high-fat diet, water accounts for 30% to 50% of the weight loss.[27]

He points out that the obese person's inability to deal with carbohydrates is due to "a block or diversion in the chain of chemical reactions leading from glucose to the release of heat and energy in his body."[28] He forcibly argues that the mental and physical mechanisms which drive an alcoholic to drink are "no different from those which drive the obese carbohydrate addict. . . . to binge on cakes and sweets. Both are forms of addiction."[29] Whereas protein and fat are not addictive, starches and sugars, especially if refined and concentrated, tend to lead to compulsive binges.[30]

Mackarness's more recent research has led him into the study of the allergy approach to mental illness. In *Not All in the Mind,* he suggests that many diseases thought to be psychosomatic are in fact "somatopsychic and have an allergic rather than an emotional basis."[31] In summary, he points out that man's nervous system was not built on starch and sugar, and, because 20th-century man tends to base his diet on refined carbohydrate, he invites "inadequately constructed and malfunctioning brain and nerves."[32]

Two American doctors, E. Cheraskin and W.M. Ringsdorf, Jr., working in similar research, point out in their book, *Psychodietetics,* that the pressures of modern society are putting increasing demands on the body, physically and mentally, but the modern diet is not sufficiently balanced to meet the stress. "Frequent dieting brings on emotional bankruptcy . . . . Now-you-see-them, now-you-don't nutrient supplies distort the brain's functioning and the mind grows metabolically frantic."[33] They, too, emphasize the fatigue of the pancreas, caused by the relentless demands made on it by refined carbohydrate. "The more sweets eaten, the more insulin is released, the lower the blood sugar levels plunge, the more sugar is craved . . . . on and on in a never-ending cycle."[34] They are attempting to persuade people to leave their addictive eating with all its incipient illnesses, physical and mental, and return to a natural diet.[35]

Dr. Atkins' Diet Revolution has sold over four million copies, a

figure which in itself shows the magnitude of the problem and the
fanaticism involved. Promising his readers that they will not be
hungry on his high-fat/high-protein diet, Dr. Atkins states:

> Stress, anxiety and emotional tension tend to make carbohydrate-
> sensitive peope fat. . . . When we are under strain, our bodies put out
> adrenalin. And adrenalin raises blood sugar levels. This in turn triggers
> off a flood of insulin, so that the blood sugar ends up lower than it
> started. . . . It is at this low point that we eat and drink for energy,
> for comfort, to rest and calm our fears, anger and tensions. Protein/
> fat combinations tend to be insulin stabilizers. . . . Unlike carbohy-
> drates, they do not dramatically affect blood sugar levels, and thus
> do not trigger the insulin flood.[36]

He also attacks caffeine in tea, coffee, and soft drinks because they
lead to an excess of insulin production.

How Stress Influences Obesity

Dr. Mackarness is indebted to Dr. Hans Selye for his studies on
stress. In *Stress Without Distress,* Selye concludes that the stages in
adaptation to stress are remarkably uniform, *irrespective of the nature of the stress.* It became evident from animal experiments that
"the same set of organ changes caused by the glandular extracts
were also produced by cold, heat, infection, trauma, haemorrhage,
nervous irritation and other stimuli."[37] In autopsy the animals all
showed swollen and discoloured adrenals, shrunken thymus, and
stomachs with bleeding ulcers. Their reaction to stress had followed
an identical pattern:

> (1) the alarm reaction in which the pituitary secretion of ACTH pre-
> cipitates the hormonal readjustment to the stress; (2) the stage of
> adaptation or resistance in which physiological homeostasis is main-
> tained under conditions of stress; (3) finally the stage of exhaustion
> in which the overtaxed glands are no longer able to carry on.[38]

Selye recognized that stress can be withstood for just so long, the
length of the resistance period depending upon the body's innate
adaptability and the intensity of the stress. Physiological and psychological abnormalities may hinder the process of adaptation. While
there are exceptions to Selye's conclusions, and while some of the
hormonal relationships are still not fully understood, researchers are
increasingly interested in discase in terms of alarm reaction and adaptation.

With specific reference to food allergy stress, Mackarness points
out that the patient may experience mental confusion, disabling

tiredness, headaches, abdominal pain, puffiness and rashes. The symptoms are generally accompanied by a craving for food or drink or cigarettes to put an end to the inner tension.[39]

The stress situation in a primarily obese child winds in a vicious circle; she tries to relieve her anxiety with food and grows fatter as a result. Like many children she imagines she is alone in some alienating way. Her imaginings, however, are well founded, for she is living in a culture intent on the beauty of thinness and therefore she carries the shadow of her peers, and even of adults.

Her damaged personality proceeds to more difficult problems in adolescence, where in our society sexuality and femininity tend to be associated with being thin. Her adaptation to adulthood develops from years of aloneness, whereas her sister with secondary obesity begins her struggle with a different relationship to her environment, to her own body image, and to a different set of fat cells. Thus the stress factor must be considered from two different points of view and two different levels of intensity.

The following chart illustrates two patterns of development: one for primary, one for secondary obesity. The stress factor is crucial—physiologically and psychologically—in both, but its variants must be taken into consideration in therapy.

DIFFERENCES IN STRESS FACTORS IN PRIMARY AND SECONDARY OBESITY

Primary (Endogenous)	Secondary (Exogenous)
1. Hypercellularity and obesity in earliest childhood.	1. Normal number of fat cells. Normal body in childhood.
2. Hypercellularity irreversible, therefore very difficult to maintain weight loss later.	2. Normal number of fat cells can be reduced in size by sensible dieting later, if necessary.
3. Overindulgence and overprotection of child may be result of fundamental rejection by parents which child unconsciously feels.	3. Child loved and allowed to grow naturally; basically secure.
4. Shy, dependent, compliant personality; often intense relationship to one parent.	4. Child allowed to grow in own space.
5. Child experiences herself as a social deformity from very beginning. Fear of being teased, fear of being rejected, fear of life. Gradual withdrawal from reality.	5. Child grows up as one of the group. Can participate in sports, dancing, fads and fashions.

6. Basic emotional insecurity. Immature ego often in unconscious. Easily falls back into regressive pattern. Tries to hold onto old ideals, rigid framework.

6. Young ego strives to grow; adjusts naturally to new situations.

7. Blocked feeling. Child cannot grow. Inability to adjust to new situations.

7. Unhampered by emotional conflict. Able to make decisions without stress.

Insecurity or need for love may develop at any age. If the immature personality cannot cope with its needs, anxiety appears. If early orientation is towards food for comfort, individual will almost certainly gain weight.

8. Feeling of passive helplessness, alternating with aggressive drive. Attempt to maintain appearance of strength and maturity. Ambivalence—striving for power, striving for affection.

8. Growing confidence in relation to own body, to maturing ego, to social situations.

9. Child eats unconsciously to compensate emotional difficulties.

9. Food is part of life.

10. By adolescence, food has acquired obsessional intensity.

10. Food is part of teenage fun.

11. Obese body makes passover into feminine maturity almost impossible. Alienation compounded.

11. Normal girl takes pride in her body, enjoys relating to men.

12. By adulthood, bad habits are engrained. Endocrine disturbances may become pathological, due to chronic fear and rage in the body, Correction becomes very difficult for both physical and psychological reasons.

12. In adulthood, other factors being equal, woman gains weight because she eats too much of the wrong food, doesn't exercise enough. Correcting habits corrects problem.

13. Dieting may not correct the obesity. Growing sense of futility and despair.

13. Weight loss leads to sense of self-respect and rejuvenation.

14. "Hormonal status of massively obese patient is markedly abnormal, more akin in many respects to that of patients with anorexia nervosa than to healthy women."[40]

14. Woman doesn't have to deal with severe hormonal difficulties unless other factors are involved or obesity is of long standing.

15. Natural life span, unless obesity is massive.

15. Shortened life span. Greater problems with diseases sometimes associated with obesity—gout, hypertension, arteriosclerosis, etc.

Selye's work continued the research of Dr. W. Walter Cannon, whose experiments in the early 20th century laid the groundwork for the study of adaptive changes in the body essential for the maintenance of life under stress. Although his work did not explore the role of the pituitary nor the adrenal cortex, as modern research has done, his findings are nonetheless valid in modern medicine. Since our analysis of the complexes in the obese individual points to an almost chronic state of fear and repressed anger, the conclusions which Cannon drew in *Bodily Changes in Pain, Hunger, Fear and Rage* are pertinent to an understanding of the body pathology which may develop. After careful experiments with animals, Cannon concluded:

> [There is] clear evidence that in pain and deep emotion, the glands do, in fact, pour out an excess of adrenin [as he then called it] [41] into the circulating blood. [42]

> [Adrenin] is capable of inducing by itself, or of augmenting the nervous influences which do induce the very changes in the viscera which accompany suffering and the major emotions. [43]

> These visceral changes which take place as a result of sympathetic stimulation are as follows: acceleration of the heart, contraction of arterioles, dilation of bronchioles, increase of blood sugar, inhibition of activity of the digestive glands, inhibition of gastro-intestinal peristalsis, sweating, discharge of adrenin, widening of the pupils, and erection of hairs. [44]

These changes occur in emotional states of fear and rage, as well as in physical states of fever and exposure to cold. Moreover, when an animal is preparing for flight or fight, the muscles of the belly wall and the diaphragm are voluntarily and antagonistically contracted, thus stiffening the trunk to support the fighting arms; the resulting increased abdominal pressure forces the blood out of the region. The distribution of the blood in the body is altered, so that while the abdominal viscera are temporarily robbed of their full blood supply, the heart, lungs, muscles, and central nervous system are well supplied. Along with the copious supply of extra blood sugar as a source of muscle energy, the body is prepared for extreme exertion. It is in such a physical crisis that binging takes place. It seems obvious that nature cannot act as a guide to a person who is so cut off from her instincts that she habitually eats when all her bodily processes are geared to fighting or fleeing rather than properly digesting food.

None of these bodily reactions in pain or intense emotion is willed movement. Through years of racial experience, these spontaneous responses in our nervous organization have been established to safeguard our survival in moments when we instinctively seek to flee or to fight. Ordinarily they are not called upon, but, if necessary, the body is ready to pour forth streams of energy. Violent emotional disturbances produce equally violent reactions in the body dynamics. Where the physical reactions to emotion and pain are not worked out by action, it is conceivable that the excessive adrenalin and sugar in the blood may have pathological effects.[45]

Cannon developed his theory further by pointing out that man differs from animals in that he has extensively developed his cerebral hemisphere. In the evolutional process, these cerebral structures have been superimposed, or grafted as it were, onto a brain stem which differs relatively little in the higher vertebrates. He concluded:

> The nervous organization for the display of rage (and the other primitive responses) both in bodily attitudes and in visceral changes, is located in an ancient portion of the brain, the optic thalamus. This region is not like the cerebral cortex where new adjustments with the outer world are constantly being made or modified. Instead, it is like the spinal cord, a place where the simpler mechanisms for orderly motions reside and where stimulation evokes fixed and uniform reflex responses.[46]

The cerebral cortex can neither cause nor prevent those stormy processes of the thalamus that produce disturbances characteristic of great excitement. *When an emotion is repressed, therefore, it is repressed only in its external manifestation.* If inhibitions are momentarily lifted, the subcortical neurones—the neurones not immediately under the control of consciousness—take over the controls and drive the individual into archaic responses.

These processes going on deep in the old part of the brain may profoundly affect the body, causing pathological disturbances. The viscera cannot be consciously controlled; moreover, they are influenced by processes associated with feeling and emotion. An emotional reaction has many of the characteristics of a reflex response; if the stimulus is ignored, it may unconsciously continue until it creates a pathological state, or it may cease to operate altogether. Since memory is held in the body, even associations may renew the original stimulus, which, though less intense, nevertheless acts on the sensitized set of responding neurones. Moreover, as Pavlov proved, associated stimuli may begin to set up a reflex action in the cerebral cortex, so that by extended associations emotional responses become subjected to more and more involved conditioned stimuli, until great complexity of affective behaviour results.

If bodily functions are persistently deranged by strong emotional reactions, then the original stimuli which evoke those reactions must

still continue, consciously or unconsciously. They persist either because they are not naturally worked out by completion of the emotional impulse, or because they are re-stimulated when completion
of the impulse is made impossible by memories, terror, or remorse
that keep the reaction alive.

The repetitive emotions that trigger the nerve impulses may cause
disastrous consequences in the organism. Because the cerebral cortex
has no control over the functions of the viscera, reason cannot check
a racing pulse by demanding that it act differently. Nor can it fill an
empty heart.

What is the significance of Cannon's work in our understanding
of obesity? Repeatedly during the Association Experiment, the
obese women, especially the primarily obese, expressed an overwhelming sense of defeat, a feeling that they were in the power of
some mysterious demonic force over which they had no control.
Fate was against them. The best they could do was accept their defeat and try to live life as fully as possible in spite of the darkness
threatening to engulf them.

Cannon's conclusions offer a physiological explanation for this
demon. The dreams of such women reveal the demonic force in the
form of serpents or prehistoric animals, turned demonic because
they are so outraged by gross insensibility to their needs. The serpent, the spirit in the body, reacts violently to the stress of modern
programming. Its rhythm is not the endless tick-tock, tick-tock, tick-
tock of the clock, nor the relentless work, work, work of the machine, nor the blind go, go, go of society. The rigid, collective consciousness it will not accept and, sooner or later, it will force the
ego to recognize its rage against enforced rational discipline. It will
transcend time even if that requires death.

Pathological Effects of Fear and Rage

Helen (51 years, 5'5", "wrong side of 180 pounds") was one of the
primarily obese women in the study. She was a "beautiful" ten-
pound baby, the oldest child of well-educated, middle class parents.
She always suspected they would have preferred a son, but she was
not overtly unwelcome. Her father, a gentle, warm, idealistic architect, found in his growing daughter the understanding and devotion
which his energetic, domineering wife could not give him. From the
beginning, Helen strove to be worthy of his love; she was his perfect
companion, his perfect student, his perfect little woman. Although
she had feared her mother, she looked back on her childhood as a
paradise.

School was the beginning of trouble. Far beyond her peers in academic ability, she was emotionally unable to relate to the rough-and-tumble of the child's world. Frightened and alone, she began to hear the mocking cries: "Fatty, Fatty, two-by-four/ Can't get through the kitchen door." She realized for the first time that she was "a social deformity." Her hypersensitivity prompted uncontrollable crying fits in the schoolyard when she was never chosen to play games. She felt her mother's shame when they went to buy clothes, and overheard her sad defence: "I don't understand it. She doesn't eat much."

"I never knew where the blow would come from," said Helen.

> I just tried to be as quiet and good as possible so no one would notice me. I lived in my own dream world. Once I struck a girl for teasing me, and then I got so angry I didn't know what I was doing and threw her over a fence. That frightened me.

When she was twelve, her father could no longer tolerate her mother's dominance and left the family, leaving Helen to care for her two younger sisters while her mother went out to work.

> I took orders from my mother. I did the shopping. I did the baking. I felt important. I was needed. I still need to be needed. I studied cookbooks to become an excellent cook. I was praised. I still need praise.

The patterns of fear and rage were deeply engrained in Helen by the age of seven. Her oversensitive nature reacted with stark terror to an external world that attacked her for her size; her fear of rejection was compensated by a desire for power. By the time she was fourteen, her metabolism was already so damaged that she was given a prescription for thyroid, on which she is still dependent and in spite of which she is always cold and tired.

Puberty and adolescence were hell. Her menstrual cycle came as a shock to her and her mother's attitude reinforced her terror and guilt. She excelled in school, but her relationship to boys was impossible. She idolized the school president from a distance and daydreamed by herself. "If I were not fat, Graham would love me." Her size became the obstacle to every joy in her life, with no understanding of the deeper problems involved. Dancing became her one passion, but after standing by the wall a few times, she turned to writing love poems or baking cakes on the night of the school dance. Sometimes the gang stopped in on the way home to sample her baking. "I was a doormat," she said. "I would do anything to win their love." At university, she tried to diet, lived on protein, but remained fat, and finally gave up her attempts to be beautiful.

> Gradually, I just couldn't care anymore. I learned to crack jokes on my-
> self before other people did. I learned to laugh at myself, but it didn't
> help the depression. I was an outsider. I became a silent, stubborn rebel.
> I knew my own point of view, and I knew I would stand and the rest of
> the world could fall.

Helen's conscious stance of strength and superiority has never reached what Cannon called the "ancient portion" of her brain. Her viscera
still lead their own fright/flight pattern of response and she feels herself victimized by a demon against which she is helpless. For twenty
years, she has lived on 900 calories a day (with a few binges and
fasts), but the scales hold relentlessly "on the wrong side of 180."
Her childless marriage ended in divorce after five years, when she
grew tired of caring for her dependent husband. She is highly respected in her profession; she carries a self-confident, calm, happy
persona.

The infantile fear/rage pattern, however, governs her existence.
She cannot cope with an adult world. Each morning begins with the
adrenalin charge when she steps on the scales. Every social situation
involving food involves the fear of losing her rigid self-control, the
fear of being rejected by men, and the rage against the silent scorn
of thin women. Her restricted diet has made her allergic to eggs,
cottage cheese, milk, coffee, and tea. She owns a wardrobe of dress-
es sizes 14-18, because she never knows what size she may be on the
night of a party.

> I look in the mirror, but I don't see myself as I am, If I am depressed, I
> see only my massive ugliness. If I am happy, I think I am statuesque. I
> have a pretty face and good hands; the rest I just cover up as best I can.

But the forgotten feminine body takes its revenge.

> Sometimes I want to lash out in a conversation. I feel outraged. I want
> to jump up or yell or sing or dance. But I say nothing. Then I feel my
> belt getting tighter, and I know it's here. The Black Thing. My body is
> swelling up, and I have to go home at once. There's nothing I can do
> about it. Sometimes I think I can't try any longer. But then I realize
> what will happen if I don't. Sometimes I just long for freedom. To die,
> to sleep, and by a sleep to say we end the whole bloody heartache.

Helen's body is repeating archaic patterns. Her fear and her rage
prepare her physically to attack, the impulses are not acted upon,
and the pathological consequences are obvious. Physically and
psychically, she is bewitched.

The psychology of a woman like Helen, during childhood and

adolescence, is very like that of an anorexic girl, however different
the physical symptoms may be. In both pathologies, the girls are repressed, too compliant, too desirous to fulfil their parents' expectations, even to fulfil their parents' unlived lives. Deprived of the freedom to live their own girlhood, they eventually rebel and tend to
become stubborn and arrogant. Both want control and seek that control through denial of food. Possession takes over in the form of
cyclic starvation and binging. The anorexic learns to win attention
and admiration through losing weight. She rejoices in her own moral
strength as she feels her skin tighten over her bones and feels herself
more acceptable in the culture. The obese adolescent who diets becomes discouraged, binges and starves without becoming thin, and
learns to experience herself as an ugly, cowardly failure in the eyes
of her parents and peer group. She lives, where her anorexic sister
may die, but she lives without hope, undermined by a deep sense of
her own moral inferiority and ultimate defeat.

The death wish in the heart of the primarily obese is not to be
overlooked. It is the other side of a fierce desire for life, for sexuality, for all the Dionysian passion for which their powerful bodies
have fitted them, but which life in this society has denied them.
Their periodic binges are an archaic expression of their defiance of
the Apollinian discipline to which they daily subject themselves. It
is significant that two of the primary cases of obesity, women who
appeared healthy and totally involved in life when we did the experiment five years ago, have since died from cancer of the female organs.
In both cases, the obesity was a concomitant of their inability to relate to their own femininity. Both were intuitives, highly intelligent,
hypersensitive. In retrospect, their comments are most poignant:

> I only know that when I hoped, I was thin; when I was in despair, I was
> fat.

> I eat and gain weight and I don't feel the tensions anymore. Now I am
> fat, but not content. I find myself wishing for the pain of dieting again,
> the agony of spirit, because in that state I feel I am growing. I feel guilty
> in this dead, fat state. There must be some way of being both thin and
> without the agony of too much awareness. It is sick to wish for the suffer-
> ing to come back just so I can feel alive.

Both fell victim to "The Black Thing," to that despair symbolized
for them in their fatness. The unknown demon, which possessed
them for a lifetime in their obesity, ultimately showed its true face
in their cancer.

Russell A. Lockhart, in "Cancer in Myth and Dream," writes:

> Perhaps in no other way does an individual experience the deepest possible meaning of 'autonomous' than in cancer attacking, seizing and consuming his life. In it, he is confronted by a truly other, a powerful *numen* threatening his very existence. . . . I consider cancer in certain forms to be related with something of the substance of one's self denied, undernourished, or cut down; something in one's psychic and bodily earth not allowed to live, not allowed to grow. Cancer lives something of life unlived.[47]

In the same article he quotes Jung:

> I have in fact seen cases where the carcinoma broke out . . . when a person comes to a halt at some essential point in his individuation or cannot get over an obstacle. Unhappily nobody can do it for him, and it cannot be forced. An inner process of growth must begin, and if this spontaneous creative activity is not performed by nature herself, the outcome can only be fatal. . . . Ultimately we all get stuck somewhere, for we are all mortal and remain but a part of what we are as a whole. The wholeness we can reach is very relative.[48]

Where the body is experienced as an obstacle that cannot be overcome, and where "spontaneous creative activity" is cut off from nature, the psyche is forced to carry an inevitably fatal load.

Clinical Approaches to Obesity

Cannon's pioneer work has been continued by specialists who have discovered how complex the homeostatic equilibrium is. In *Emotions and Bodily Changes,* Dr. Flanders Dunbar summarizes clinical experiments and concludes:

> The endocrine-hormonal system has been recognized as the translator of the tempo of the nervous system into the tempo of metabolism and vice versa. . . . Repeated research has proven that nature intended all emotions to lead to immediate physical activity and when this does not occur the blood is poisoned. . . . When the cause which has originated this anxiety state has been removed, then the condition can be successfully treated by the bacteriologist and endocrinologist.[49]

Researchers tend to agree that although endocrine dysfunction does not cause neurosis and psychosis, it does intensify the constitutional predisposition to them. Treatment by endocrine therapy is merely cutting the weeds off at the surface without eradicating the roots. The sooner the roots are pulled, the less danger there is of permanent damage organically and mentally. Prolonged conflict causes persistent disturbance in endocrine secretion and may cause secondary pathological changes in the organs. Only a personality relatively free from conflict will have harmonious metabolic homeostasis.

Much research has focused on the eating habits of the obese. Researchers at the College of Medicine in Vermont in 1971 attempted to study obesity by asking normal student volunteers to overeat deliberately. They discovered that these students could gain barely 10% of their weight and maintain their usual activities. In order to continue their experiments, they decided to enrol volunteers from the state prison who could remain physically inactive, and therefore gain more weight. From this research, it became clear that gaining weight is not purely a matter of self-discipline, but rather "a deep-seated and usually inherited problem of physiologic control."[50] Because these volunteers all lost their gained weight as quickly as obese people regain it, they concluded that

> heritable derangement of obesity may be an overriding disturbance at the level at which the Central Nervous System is set. This could be an exaggeration of those mechanisms to promote food storage of energy which had survival value for our remote ancestors, but which in an exaggerated form become a liability to us in our affluent society.[51]

One of the most decisive findings in the study was that "spontaneously obese persons required less than half as many calories to maintain the obese state as did the experimental subjects."[52]

Dr. Richard Nisbett suggests from his experiments that many "overweight" people who are dieting in an attempt to conform with the insurance companies' ideal charts, are actually underweight and hungry all the time. He goes on to show that a kind of functional lesion of the ventromedial hypothalamus takes place in an animal deprived of food for seven days. This lesion produces an animal that eats more, eats more rapidly, is hyper-responsive to food, far more fearful and given to rage than normal, and is inactive and hyposexual. He concludes: "The parallels to hunger and to the behaviour of the obese human seem too marked to be coincidental."[53] As yet, however, the complex set of interconnected circuits in the brain which constitute the "appestat" is still a mystery.

Inadequate as this summary must be, it is enough to illustrate the complexity of the problem and the amount of research devoted to it. Tepperman confidently predicts that in not too many years, obesity will be regarded as a symptom, like hypertension or fever, and that it will be possible to classify obese patients into various pathophysical categories. "The most impressive single fact about the experimental obesities is their variety, i.e., the fact that animals get fat for quite different reasons."[54]

Jung's Concept of Psyche and Body

In turning from Cannon's pioneer work to that of C.G. Jung, one discovers that while Cannon was working on the involuntary physiological responses to fear and rage, Jung was working on the psychological responses to intense emotions in the Association Experiment. Both scientists were proving the existence of two systems in the individual—one voluntary, one autonomous. Jung, however, was to arrive at certain conclusions that give to Cannon's work a teleological meaning that goes not only beyond Cannon's understanding of the phenomena he was investigating, but also beyond the work of Freud, whose respect for Jung dated from his important work on the Association Experiment.

Jung was eventually to conclude that the various bodily symptoms were messages from the psyche itself. They therefore could be given a symbolic meaning, the key to which was most immediately accessible in dream images. The dream served as an intermediary between the physiological and the psychic, yoking them together, just as projections pointing outward to objects were yoked to symbols pointing inward to Self. For Jung, the healing power resided in a conscious awareness of the symbolic nature of the dream, which provided the psychic meaning of those body symptoms by which the spirit struggled to communicate its condition and its needs. The body via the dream images was yoked to spirit. To become conscious of the body and its operations was to become conscious of the spirit. The individuation process, therefore, could also be observed in the body. Bearing this in mind, obesity must be understood in terms of the symbol. In that understanding lies the treatment and the possibility of healing.

In his early work, Jung was able to ascertain the strong feeling tone in a complex, along with certain physical reactions, by observing the curves made by a galvanometer attached to a volunteer in response to a given stimulus. At the same time he used a pneumograph to study the respiratory curve. He found that there did not seem to be the depth of relationship between the respiratory function and the unconscious emotions that there was between the sweat glandular system and these emotions. He concluded:

> Perhaps the emotions of the unconscious, roused up by questions or words that strike into the buried complexes of the soul, reveal themselves in the galvanometer curve, while the pneumographic curve is comparatively unaffected. Respiration is an instrument of consciousness. You can control it voluntarily while you cannot control the galvanometer curve.[55]

Like Cannon, Jung went on to explore the power that these constellations, conscious and unconscious, can have over an individual because of the force they exert upon associations.

> The complex robs the ego of light and nourishment, just as a cancer robs the body of its vitality. The sequelae of the complex are briefly as follows: Diminution of the entire psychic energy, weakening of the will, loss of objective interest and of power of concentration and of self-control, and the rise of morbid hysterical symptoms. These results can also manifest themselves in associations.[56]

Jung recognized that the power of the complex could have pathological results in the body:

> It is possible that in the disposition to dementia praecox affectivity brings about certain irreparable organic disturbances, as for instance metabolic toxins.[57]

Repeatedly he emphasized that it was not the intellect but the emotions that were the chief factor in determining these associations, and that "all affective processes are more or less clearly connected with physical manifestations."[58]

If we imagine Cannon's animal world of flight or fight storming in our viscera, either as a direct reaction or as one triggered by association, we can relate such violent responses to Jung's affective elements of the complex. He defined a "complex" as

> a collection of imaginings, which, in consequence of [its] autonomy, is relatively independent of the central control of the consciousness, and at any moment liable to bend or cross the intentions of the individual.[59]

When the body is holding the complex, it then becomes our most immediate access to the problem. Symptoms, such as Helen described when her fear or rage suddenly made her body swell, are the products of the deliberate intention of the unconscious to cross the conscious intention of the individual. The "demon" that she experiences, physically and psychically, does in fact "possess" her because the complex is usurping the power of her conscious ego.[60]

Forty years of intensive observation brought Jung to a much deeper understanding of the relationship between psyche and soma. Speaking of a dissociated secondary consciousness, he pointed out that it cannot cross the threshold into ego-consciousness because it "represents a personality-component which has not been separated from ego-consciousness by mere accident, but . . . owes its separation to definite causes."[61] One cause may be the repression of dissociated material because of its incomplete nature; another may be that the dissociated material has never entered into consciousness because consciousness has no way of understanding it. However, "because there is in both cases sufficient energy to make it potentially conscious, the secondary subject does in fact have an effect upon ego-consciousness."[62] This effect manifests symbolically in the symptoms. Generally, these powerful repressed contents are not really repressed, but rather, like the gods of the primitives, have not yet been made conscious.

Jung recognized that we experience the psychic process apart from its relation to organic matter, but as a psychologist he was interested in the totality of these experiences. This totality he termed "psychoid."[63] Further, Jung's view was that the unconscious possesses a "consciousness" of its own, a second psychic system coexisting with consciousness.[64]

The psychic processes which we are able to observe and experience are linked with the body, and therefore must have a share in its instincts or be the result of the actions of those instincts. Using the phrasing of Pierre Janet, Jung concluded:

> The instinctual base governs the *partie inférieure* of the function [the organism], while the *partie supérieure* corresponds to its predominantly "psychic" component. The *partie inférieure* proves to be the relatively unalterable, automatic part of the function, and the *partie supérieure,* the voluntary and alterable part.[65]

The physiological aspect, the *partie inférieure,* seems to be bound up with the hormones; its function is compulsive by nature and is therefore called a "drive." The psychic aspect, the *partie supérieure,* has lost its compulsive character, can be subjected to the will, and even applied contrary to the instinct.

In the psychic sphere, the life force can be freed from its instinctual compulsive form at the bottom, and at the top, energized by other determinants, it eventually ceases "to be oriented by instinct in the original sense, and attains a so-called 'spiritual' form."[66] The motive power of the instinct is not substantially altered, but its mode of application is, for it may be masking a sense of direction other than a biological one.

This process can be seen in spiritual fasting, for example, where the denial of food is accompanied by spiritual disciplines. Without spiritual motivation, a person undergoing a fast will almost certainly suffer intense physical and psychic anxiety. But if the fast is recognized as a purification rite and reinforced with spiritual food, body and spirit come together on a new level of inner integration. An aberration of fasting appears in the anorexic girl who determinedly puts herself through ritual vomiting rather than give up the "high" she experiences through starvation. Without the spiritual food, however, body and spirit are dangerously separated.

The life force is ultimately motivated by instinct; according to Jung, the will "cannot coerce the instinct, nor has it power over the spirit. . . . Spirit and instinct are by nature autonomous and both limit in equal measure the applied field of the will."[67] From this point of view,

> psyche is essentially conflict between blind instinct and will. . . . Where instinct predominates, *psychoid* processes set in which pertain to the sphere of the unconscious as elements incapable of consciousness.[68]

Katherine's Serpent Dream

The dream of Katherine (48 years, 5'9", 165 pounds), who was in analysis at the time of the experiment, will illustrate how valid Jung's concepts are.

Katherine had been very successful in her professional career, but was gradually being handicapped by cyclic edema for which sleep was the only medicine. This symptom is defined as "recurrent episodes of swelling of the whole body with water retention at times of stress."[69] Superficially, edema looks like obesity. The dream was as follows:

> I am a priestess in a temple. A festival is about to take place. Near the ceiling in the back wall, the stones form an open space in the shape of a cross. On the altar, I am arranging roses—white and pink roses—so that they form a cross exactly where the sun shining through the wall will illuminate them. All is in readiness except the central flowers. People begin to arrive; we await the priest who will begin the rites.
>
> An old man grasps my hand and takes me down ancient stone stairs, covered in moss. I do not know this place. It is very dark, but I can distinguish a grotto and water, and a huge twenty-foot pitch-black snake beside a water wheel [Figure 1, page 65]. It thrusts its head back and forth in a rhythmical movement which should be hitting the spokes to make the wheel go around. But the creature is in agony, aimlessly striking into the darkness; it knows it isn't hitting the wheel. The old man says, "It supplies the energy for the temple." I attempt to move the wheel towards the snake, but the old man pulls me back and I realize how dangerous the snake is.
>
> I feel guilty because keeping the temple in running order seems to be my duty as priestess. This problem is beyond me. The rites must be postponed because the prayers cannot reach heaven until the wheel is turning again. The old man watches me in silence.

This was the dream of a well-organized, extraverted, and highly intuitive woman, who was well adapted to the collective religious values, but with a deep sense of her own personal commitment. In the dream, she is responsible for the care of the temple, the sacred precinct, which physiologically may be interpreted as her body. In the *partie supérieure,* all appears to be in readiness for an epiphany. The light of consciousness shines in a cross formation on a cross of opposites—white and pink roses—the flowers of Aphrodite, symbolizing physical passion, and of the Virgin Mary, symbolizing spiritual passion.

The totality of the mandala on the altar cannot be completed because, while all appears ordered, personally and collectively, there is a serious problem underneath. The powerful Kundalini energy is cut off from the transformer which circulates energy in the temple. Either she has repressed her instincts or she has never become conscious of them.

The foundations of the temple are made of stone but covered with moss through lack of use. The depth of the grotto and her total unawareness of its existence suggest that she has inherited the powerful instinctual energy, but that the god has not yet been made conscious. The serpent god has a consciousness of its own, for it knows that it should be connected to the wheel and its futile efforts make it writhe in agony. Growing in the darkness, it has attained a huge size, and its mercurial power could prove very dangerous to a novitiate. But the wise old man, representing an aspect of the Self, has led her to this grotto because he wants her to be whole. He protects her when she foolishly (using the logic of the upper world) attempts to move the wheel to the snake. The healing serpent in the grotto can be amplified from ancient Epidaurus to modern Lourdes.

The symptom itself was flooding of her body with water. In her early twenties, she had lost almost 100 pounds through will-power and dancing, and still organized her life so that she made constant demands on her energy, physically and mentally. The edemic syndrome was gradually increasing in severity. It would appear that while she was able to conquer her weight problem by an act of will, and control her life by rigid diet and organized activity, she was now having to face the fact that her will could neither coerce her instinct, nor have power over her spirit. (The prayers could not rise to heaven until the wheel was turning.) The unconscious manifested in her physical body in water and forced her to return to itself in sleep. The tears she was unable to shed by day, she wept in her dreams.

Figure 1. The serpent by the water wheel.
(Original in colour, painted by the dreamer)

The Self was using her body to force her to recognize that her internal dam had to give way. The too-disciplined, too-logical, unflowing way of life had to give place to the more feminine flood, which could only be regulated when the wheel of life was properly connected to its own energy source. The Kundalini serpent was arrested at the *swadhistana chakra* (the kidney chakra), her feelings were blocked, and the physical symptom was kidney failure.

The motive power of the serpent seemed to be a biological one, and on this level it was, for she had to take care of her sick body; its real sense of direction, however, was towards the sun, the *sahasrara crown chakra,* for the integrity of the temple and the efficacy of the prayers depended on that totality. The mandala could not be completed without that connection. Until she went into analysis, she felt herself at the mercy of a demon. The psychoid process, as the messenger of the spirit, forced her to listen to her own Being. (Katherine's subsequent development is illustrated in her Crowned Serpent dream, Chapter V.)

The dream also shows the affinity of archetype with instinct, although they are polar opposites. "Psychic processes," Jung wrote, "seem to be balances of energy flowing between spirit and instinct."[70] Using the simile of the spectrum, he continued as follows:

> The dynamism of instinct is lodged as it were in the infra-red part of the spectrum, whereas the instinctual image lies in the ultra-violet part. . . . The archetype is more accurately characterized by violet, for, as well as being an image in its own right, it is at the same time a *dynamism* which makes itself felt in the numinosity and fascinating power of the archetypal image. The realization and assimilation of instinct never takes place at the red end, i.e. by absorption into the instinctual sphere, but only through integration of the image which signifies and at the same time evokes the instinct, although in a form quite different from the one we meet on the biological level.[71]

He stressed that the archetype must not be confused with the archetypal image. "The archetype as such is a psychoid factor that belongs, as it were, to the invisible, ultra-violet end of the psychic spectrum."[72]

> It is not only possible but fairly probable, even, that psyche and matter are two different aspects of one and the same thing. . . . Just as the "psychic infra-red," the biological instinctual psyche, gradually passes over into the physiology of the organism and thus merges with its chemical and physical conditions, so the "psychic ultraviolet," the archetype, describes a field which exhibits none of the peculiarities of the physiological and yet, in the last analysis, can no longer be regarded as psychic, although it manifests itself psychically.[73]

The psychoid archetype (Figure 2) is almost impossible to explain because it is essentially a mystery, but its numinosity can be experienced through both body and psyche. Its healing power can radiate through the person who reveres it as a visible, luminous quality which seems rooted in some divine stillness.

INSTINCTS		ARCHETYPES
infra-red ————————	experience	———————— ultra-violet
(**Physiological:** body symptoms, instinctual perceptions, etc.)		(**Psychological:** ideas, conceptions, dreams, images, fantasies, etc.)

Figure 2. The psychoid archetype.

Any woman who takes herself seriously must accept the responsibility of knowing and loving her body. This is the hardest task for the obese woman, especially if it has been her enemy all her life. On her deepest level, she feels either that she has betrayed it, or it has betrayed her. What she sees in the mirror is a parody of herself. If she chooses to ignore it, the Magna Mater will take more violent revenge. If she tries to face it, she may eventually see her own shadow, become aware of what is in her own unconscious, and then take a strong enough ego position to react psychologically to difficulties in her environment. Only when she can consciously recognize her emotions and begin to deal with life directly will her reactions cease to appear in physical form as a symptom.

Some knowledge of the scientific research now available may encourage her. Certainly, some awareness of the complexity of the biochemical reactions in her body in response to her own emotions, conscious and unconscious, will bring her to an appreciation of this magnificent creation. She may learn to listen to its wisdom. This is her body. This is her greatest gift, pregnant with information she has refused to acknowledge, grief she thought she had forgotten, and joy she has never known. If she can love her own *massa confusa* and dedicate herself to its mystery, she may one day find herself smiling from her mirror. She may even come to trust the voice that quietly asks, "Know ye not that your body is the temple of the Holy Ghost which is in you, which ye have of God, and ye are not your own?" (1 Corinthians 6:19)

CHAPTER III

THREE CASE STUDIES

> . . . I have heard the key
> Turn in the door once and turn once only
> We think of the key, each in his prison
> Thinking of the key, each confirms a prison
> Only at nightfall . . .
>
> —T.S. Eliot, *The Waste Land*

Studying three cases in further depth may help to clarify the relationship of the complexes, and the relationship between body and psyche discussed in general terms in the first two chapters. While gathering material for this study, it became clear to me that the distance between obesity and anorexia nervosa is little more than a fine line and, especially in a young woman, a dividing line that must be recognized and respected. In fact, in dreams the shadow of an obese woman may appear as an anorexic girl, and vice versa.

Two young analysands—one overweight, one anorexic—generously agreed to share their fantasies and experiences. The third case is a further analysis of the material of the edemic woman whose serpent dream was presented in Chapter II. I include her material because it shows how one symptom will replace another if the original cause is not removed and clearly illustrates the psychoid nature of the archetype.

MARGARET (24 years, 5'5", 187 pounds)

Margaret's appearance conveyed the ambivalence that many obese women unconsciously emit. Her body was awkward, uncoordinated, covered over by a tent dress; her hands were alert, beautifully shaped, and most expressive when she talked. Her skin would make any woman envious; her eyes danced with laughter and tears. She breathed the fiery dragon out one nostril and the Blessed Mother out the other. She told all she could as fast as she could with dramatic flair and more than a touch of the Blarney. Momentarily, she could switch from a Shakespearian wench into a potentially beautiful woman. Although she was twenty-four she looked seventeen. She balanced precariously on the tightrope of the opposites so widely apart within her: joy/grief; spirituality/sexuality; God/Devil; power/inferiority; aesthetic sensitivity/coarse sensuality.

Raised in a family of eight, she was the middle girl. She had known privation as a child because her father, "an honest working man," was a heavy drinker. Her mother, determined to do her best for her children, managed the household, and by her sly remarks, turned her daughter against her father. Margaret grew up believing that her mother was a lady, always immaculate herself and clean in her housekeeping, "a wonderful Christian soul." Only later did she realize that "Mother pretended to love, but she didn't really. She acted kind but there was no spontaneity in her response." Both her mother and grandmother had nervous breakdowns after the births of some of their children, a fact which frightened Margaret. All her mother's unlived life was focussed on her because she was such a good child, so beautiful, so intelligent. By giving her the best possible education in a Catholic school administered by strict nuns, the mother hoped she would find a good job and marry well.

She came into analysis because she could not stay on a diet. There was no history of obesity in the family, nor were her siblings fat. She had been a thin, sensitive child. Her menstrual cycle did not begin until she was seventeen, at which time she became a secret eater. After gaining thirty pounds, she dieted and her periods stopped. "I don't know whether I couldn't eat, or didn't. I got sick at the thought of sex." After hospital care, her periods returned along with the weight. "I thought constantly of food. I could not control myself, although I felt guilty eating at all. When I got fat, I stayed in bed most of the time, except to creep out for food." Finally she left home, but had great difficulty finding a job that was good enough for her. "I was so scared I ate every time things went bad. They were always bad. I couldn't stand men. As soon as I felt men liked me, I turned against them."

Several characteristics of both obesity and anorexia are clear: the early identification with the mother, the unrealistic hopes of the parent pinned on the child, her infantile attitude towards sexuality, her food problem coinciding with the onset of menstruation. Unable to discriminate between her projections and outer reality, her infantile imagination fed on self-deceptions.

After three weeks in analysis, she began to lose weight. She reported two repetitive fantasies: she would kill herself if she got any fatter; she was afraid she might become a whore. "It would serve me right," she said. "I know why I want to be thin." The madonna/whore complex was related to both the sexual and the eating complexes. She wanted to be like the Virgin Mary (as her mother had hoped), but on her way to church she was often waylaid by several chocolate bars. These bars usually became a binge. Her inner dialogue went something like this:

> *Virgin Margaret:* I want to be filled with beauty, light, love. Love—BAH! I hate men. If I am fat, they don't touch me. I hate priests too. They are men underneath their skirts. Don't want Mass.
>
> *Piggy Maggie:* I certainly don't. Those young priests are all hypocrites. I want chocolates. I want to be loved. I hate them all. I want enough sugar to fall asleep, to escape from the whole impossible mess.

Her tiny ego could barely balance between "the terrible joy of the presence of God" and the crashing depression when God cursed her. Her faith became a hindrance rather than a point of orientation for her fading ego. In an attempt to compensate for her growing sense of inferiority when she was flooded by unconscious material, she would bargain with God to help her. When she lost no weight, she refused to bow the knee to such a cruel tyrant. That she might have to obey nature's laws never occurred to her. When the unconscious turned hostile, she would come to sessions with a white and expressionless face. "I'm not here," she would say. "It's The Thing." Her love of the Virgin was her only real solace and even that was contaminated by thoughts of rigid nuns "who probably had their breasts and hair cut off."

When she lost a few pounds she was so happy she went to buy clothes. She imagined she was slim and tried to squeeze into a size 14 when she was in fact an 18. Her mental image of her body was totally unrelated to the facts. When she couldn't get into the dress, she flew into a rage and bought food for a binge. A binge meant going to her flat alone, locking the door, not answering the telephone and eating from Friday night until Monday morning, wolfing cereals, brown sugar, cream, and stolen cakes "because I need them":

I'm not there when I eat. I eat like an animal, not with proper dishes. I enjoy the food at first. Then Darkness begins to come. I feel Darkness all around me. Then I get scared and real Darkness is right behind me. It is Death. I realize I am fighting for my life. I don't care whether I live. Something else takes over. I cannot think. I cannot feel. I cannot pray. If only I could be free.

Out of this hell, she emerged on Monday morning and kept going to her job until Friday, with compulsive night eating.

For a girl like Margaret, the analyst must be ready to carry the projection of the Self, because she is unrelated to her own inner core. She is trying to find her own values, her own feelings, in the confidence of the analyst's love. She hungers for a love she has never known, a love that can accept her "in all her rottenness." But she also hungers for a life she has never known and that hunger may manifest in extreme possessiveness and jealousy. Marie-Louise von Franz speaks of this quality in amplifying the symbolism of the wolf:

> In the dreams of modern women the wolf often represents the animus, or that strange devouring attitude women can have when possessed by the animus . . . . the wolf represents that strange indiscriminate desire to eat up everybody and everything . . . . which is visible in many neuroses where the main problem is that the person remains infantile because of an unhappy childhood. . . . It is not really that *they* want it, *it* wants it. Their "it" is never satisfied, so the wolf also creates in such people a constant, resentful dissatisfaction. . . . The wolf is called *lykos,* light. The greed when mastered or directed onto its right goal is *the* thing.[74]

This caged, archaic energy is revealed in one of Margaret's animal dreams:

> There are four lions in a cage—male, female, and two cubs. I was scared but my eldest sister was with me and I felt safe. I didn't want to show my fear. One came over to touch me and I screamed at her to keep him away. She laughed and said they were quite harmless.

Lions are animals of power and lust, but the shadow sister is able to recognize the power as harmless because in life she is able to love without the will to power. The potential is in that love and in the two cubs, for the lion is a symbol of spiritual power as well.

Unhappy with her gradual progress, which she could see only in terms of weight loss, Margaret began taking amphetamines on her doctor's prescription. Immediately, she became euphoric with artificial energy and hope. In two months she lost over twenty-four pounds, thus altering the symptom but not the disease. With her

emerging beauty, the problem of her weak feminine ego and her
fear of men became obvious. She had been trying to relate to her
body through the mirror, through exercise and through dance, but
her feminine feeling was barely budding. She longed for a boyfriend,
but when men touched her she became hostile. Afterwards she was
sorry but felt they deserved what they got. "I can't help it. That's
the way I am. At least I can admit it. I know it is evil but I don't
feel guilty." Her question now became, "If I do get thin, what have
I got then? I am a raging volcano. I am beside myself." Her dreams,
too, were full of storms, fires, and herself helpless at the wheel of a
high-powered car racing towards cliffs. Although she realized the
effects of the amphetamines, she refused to stop taking them.

Then nightmares began. The following dream reveals Margaret's
anorexic shadow:

> I was in bed with my eldest sister when I heard footsteps on the stairs.
> We turned on the light and saw someone running up the steps. She
> was immensely tall and abnormally thin. Her face was long and her
> two eyes huge in her face; they shone like cat's eyes. She was really
> frightening. She seemed like a wild animal in one way, and in another
> like a strange, unearthly being. I was terrified of her and wanted to
> kill her, but feared she was too strong for me. My sister cornered her
> behind a door. She never uttered a sound—just knelt there with a
> haunted look like a trapped animal. I woke up sweating and shaking
> with fear.

Her starving body and threatened feminine are looking her straight
in the eye in the dream. Her fear of deprivation of both love and
food is haunting her and although she would like to kill it, she fears
it is too strong for her. The amphetamines were driving her towards
the breaking point because she was not ready to take on the mature
feminine role; the extremities of the conflict were intensified without food and by the effect of the drug. She became "possessed."
She would plan to go to a party, buy a dress, fix her hair, and arrive
on the wrong day. Other times, she would binge the day before, so
her body was distended beyond the dress. The negative parental
images would not allow her to have fun nor to go out into life. It
became a cycle of rebellious aggression, followed by hopeless depression.

Finally, a dream suggested that God had cursed her for a purpose
and maybe she should deal with it naturally. She stopped the drug.
She immediately gained several pounds. The relationship of power
to weight is clear in her comments at this time:

Now look what you've made me do. Still, I am happy in these rages. I see things in a special way. I love them in their ugliness. I love my big powerful self. The world can't tell me what to do. I don't need you or anyone else to help me. I do see the possibility of good coming out of evil because in this mood, I am most strong, most creative, most energetic. I talked to the lion. I told him to stop and after a long fight, he did, but it killed something in me. I didn't want to live anymore. I gave up. Better to have him prowling around than dead. At least I'm alive when I'm eating.

Margaret's conscious perfectionist attitude was compensated by her unconscious feelings of inferiority which took their revenge in greed and longing for power. Her identification with beauty, goodness, and light led to unbearable confrontations with reality, and further binging and depressions. By being driven into her own Darkness, she was forced to deal with her own earth which was telling her that she was not all-powerful, nor perfect, but a human being who had to accept her limitations and imperfections. Thus the symptom was forcing her to deal with the reality which she despised. Nature worked in direct compensation: the more inflated her fantasies, the blacker her Darkness. So long as she screamed out against the unjust God and defiantly rejected nature, she was driven by her dark animus, and forced to feed him.

Exactly nine months after her analysis began, Margaret attended midnight Mass on Christmas Eve—alone, without family, without friends. She had chosen to do so because she was fat and afraid and ashamed. The hole she had dug for herself terrified her. For the first time she experienced her real suffering. "I have missed my whole life, dreaming of the great person my mother wanted me to be. My whole life is a lie." That insight forced her to earth and her own responsibility for her own life.

In clinical terms, the components in Margaret's psychology relevant to this study seem to be a power-driven negative animus, a frightened persona, a weak feminine ego threatened by powerful opposites, a pathological emotionality, and a narcissistic immaturity. She had neither a strong father, nor a feminine mother, thus her model of masculinity was her mother's animus. Without an authentic masculine principle, and without her feminine instinct, she had no inner voice to tell her to care for her body and stop binging.

With almost no experience of Eros, she had developed very little ability to relate and thus when the void of her feelings opened, her fierce animus demanded food. Unable to relate to him physically or psychically, she gave him the only food of love she understood—cereal and sweets. These energized her until she again saw reality in the mirror; then she fled into fantasies—fantasies of what love and men should be, the fantasies of an adolescent. This fantasy world allowed her to avoid all conflict and genuine feeling, allowed her to indulge in megalomanic visions of herself as powerful, rich, well-educated, indispensable to other people's lives, thus compensating her conscious attitude of being powerless, ugly, and alone. The aggression which she felt against a God who had put her in this position she turned against herself. The spiritual food for which she desperately yearned was profaned by equally desperate eating. Undefended by a spiritual animus, she fell under the spell of a demon who threatened to lure her into death.

The displacement of the sexual complex onto food began at puberty. By nineteen, "the thin, dirty whore" shadow was firmly entrenched against "the fat, pure Madonna" persona; the negative animus claimed both for his bride. Her inferior, introverted sensation allowed her to fall into a dissociation between body and spirit. Her unconscious body became her hated shadow which she could not look at clothed or naked. Hilde Bruch in *Eating Disorders* states:

> The lack of will power [in the obese] is related to their inability to perceive their bodily needs. Fat people tend to talk about their bodies as external to themselves. They do not feel identified with this bothersome and ugly thing they are condemned to carry through life, and in which they feel confined or imprisoned.[75]

When Margaret first lost weight, she kept touching herself as if to be sure she was still there. It was puzzling that although she was small until she was seventeen, her body image was large. Was her body mirroring her inflated fantasies? Or were the fantasies so inflated, her body had to hold her down? Certainly, her body was the one thing that forced her to reality.

Her repetitive dreams of cats, black dogs, and dark men suggested a sexual origin to her symptoms, which could be connected with the matriarchal line of childbirth problems in her family, and with her madonna rejection of her whore. Discussing hysteria, Jung wrote: "What the patient is yearning for is doubtless the Man . . . . The fear of the sexual future and all its consequences is too great for the patient to decide to abandon her illness."[76]

The combination of three dynamic complexes—religion, sexuality, and food—created its own abnormal autonomy in Margaret. It would appear that the energy in the religious and sexual complexes, both charged with intense feeling tones, was displaced onto food. Her fear of being carried off into the Darkness was related to her weak ego and her fear of annihilation, a fear connected with both death and sexual intercourse. The power of these three complexes constellated what Jung might call "a new morbid personality,"[77] which moved only in the direction of being fat. This second personality threatened to devour the ego and force it into a secondary role. Only when the *lykos,* the light, is directed onto its right goal can the greed of the wolf be transformed into the creative energy necessary to dispel the Darkness.

What does Margaret's symptom symbolize? On one level, her fatness protects her against men. Her negative animus cocoons her from the world. Although part of her naturally longs for a lover, the other part, who knows the annihilating power of her negative animus only too well, fears masculine aggression. Because her relationship to the masculine was through her mother's animus with all its ambitions and illusions, she has no strong masculine voice to bring order to her life, to say NO to binging; instead, her masculine voice is insatiable in its demands. The feminine child within needs the fat body to protect her from any mature male and from the responsibility of mature feminine feeling.

On another level, her size mirrors her inflation, a balloon full of fantasies of her own possibilities, her intelligence, her beauty, her indispensability; it masks the reality of her failure, fear, and guilt. It is an insulating wall against a world in which she neither understands nor is understood.

As a healing symptom, her fat body acting as the messenger of the spirit is forcing her to wholeness. She has to come out of her fantasies and look at reality in the mirror. There she may see the truth behind those animal drives for food, and learn to know her own feminine nature where those drives will be transformed into a human search for love and a spiritual search for serenity. Instead of blindly fighting her whore and becoming fatter, she may relax into the feminine, and release her true madonna.

ANNE (22 years, 5'6", 132 pounds)

Anne was the older of two daughters born to a prosperous business-man and his schoolteacher wife. Her father travelled during the week but when he returned, life was always festive. He and his daughter had wonderful times together:

> I was his favourite child. Mother says I am like him in my intelligence, my sense of humour, and my meanness. My grandmother couldn't abide my father's love for me. He was her baby. He always wanted to get away from her and from society. He left us when I was five. Now he is in a hospital for alcoholism.

From the beginning she was an imaginative, highly creative, very intelligent child who refused to live life the neighbourhood way and refused to play with dull, expensive toys.

> I preferred hardship games like war refugees or Anne Frank. On Sunday evenings I asked for cold beans out of a can. I always felt there was a conspiracy to keep my real identity away from me. I believed my real father was an emperor who allowed me to come into this life as a trial. He watched to see with what dignity I took punishment from these peons. They were his servants. Sometimes he was meshed in with God. I really suspected that behind every mirror something was watching. Worlds behind worlds. Things are not what they seem.
>
> I was concerned to be good, but I was so full of energy and so curious and so full of ideas, I seemed to be a rebel. The teacher tied me to the desk at school. I wrote plays for the neighbourhood kids, and my sister always acted in them until she was about eight. Then she rebelled against me. She never got spanked. I was spanked so much my mother thought she would murder me. "Eat this meal I prepared for you," she'd say. "No," I'd reply. She took a hard line with me; she said I had to learn the facts of life. She said I was so hot-tempered only my family could love me.

Anne was normal weight until seventeen, no eating problems, no menstruation problems. She hated her stepfather. She was at the top of her class, but began to realize she was socially immature in relation to her peers.

> The world seemed infinitely possible to me until I was sixteen. Then I lost my will. At seventeen, I felt doomed. I became anxious to be mature. I wanted things to go well, so I tried to be compliant but I was always in trouble with authority. I tried to speak the truth as I saw it, but my best intentions always backfired. The real thing I could not say; either it was not heard or it wouldn't be believed.
>
> The climax came when I was editor of the school newspaper. I had what I thought was a brilliant idea for an editorial. The principal

called me to his office, censored my article and told me to "grow up."
He said it wasn't valid to be angry; it wasn't valid to have instincts
like mine, always wanting to do battle. I felt vicious. I decided to try
the goodness of self-discipline. I would not eat. I was mad at every-
body, mostly myself, because I couldn't figure things out. Sex was
free; drugs were open. I couldn't handle either and I didn't care
about social skills. Not eating seemed a good way of getting back at
myself because I couldn't cope with myself. I couldn't grow up into
that world.

Nobody understood. I couldn't make the doctor hear. The hair on
my head fell out, but other hair grew all over my body. My period
stopped. My weight dropped to ninety pounds very quickly. Just before I went into the hospital, I had a premonition quieter than sleep.
It was a repetitive dream both waking and asleep. I was in a high
white bed in a white room. The blinds were pulled, the atmosphere
sepulchral. I was small in the big bed. I would shrink away, shrink into
nothing. I didn't want death consciously. I kept my consciousness
away from the idea of where this was ultimately leading. I wanted the
vacation of non-stimulation, quieter than sleep. While I was starving,
everything had become too acute and I longed to get away. Dying
seemed the only way of beating the system.

Then I got angry and said everything I felt about my stepfather.
I said I felt no anger towards my mother. It wasn't her fault. I feel
anger toward her now, but I cannot express it. I always see the reason,
and therefore I can't get angry; the emotion seethes in me. I don't
know how to express anger in an adult way.

One day I decided I wasn't trying to kill myself. I saw I had to decide on the side of dying or living. I decided to live. I wanted to take
life-affirming steps. If denying food was denying life, then the more I
ate, the more I was affirming life. I went overboard and gained thirty-
five pounds in one year. I wanted granola, milk and sugar, ice cream
and yogurt. All milk things. I wanted filling things, good things.
Gradually my energy came back through swimming. That released
me to write. I was compulsive about learning, not that I cared about
the grades, but I did care about following an idea through to get the
most out of it. Living in a women's college was very difficult because
they were fanatic about what they would and would not eat. Their
values were based on vanity, shallowness, concern for the world's
point of view.

Gradually she gained a foothold in life. She graduated from university, but life and food are still a problem.

Sometimes when I feel anxious, I feel I am rising off the earth. I feel
ants and butterflies are in me carrying me up. I can't endure it. I wish
I could put a rock in my stomach to hold me down, to feel grounded
in life, to bring me back to a place from which I could go out again.
I would like to get down to me. Often I dream of looking for land-
marks as to where to go, how to handle life. I look for life-affirming

things. When I eat, I just keep on eating. I am trying to reach right into the centre of life. I don't think I could go on without those periods of suspended self-discipline. I just can't keep saying, "Don't, don't, don't eat this, exercise that, obey the rules." When I can't take the pain any longer, I always eat with the idea of going to sleep. I want to saturate myself, to come down heavy, warm, concrete, and comfortable. I need to give myself free rein, and though the path is not a noble one, and one I don't wish to persevere in, I need it. I bring things to a crisis. When I can't eat anymore and can't sleep anymore, I have to get up and go on.

Eating is both comfort and self-destruction. Sometimes food makes me feel that life isn't terrible. Other times I overeat just to set up a wall of flesh between me and other beings. I don't want to be a sexual, bodily being. I want to be zero, a blob, and forget the world. Being "loggy" is being in a state of sweet lethargy, the opposite of being a pincushion for every stimulus. Sometimes I am so pinned I don't know what to do. My heart won't break; I wish it would. It's not a problem of having a broken spirit. It's a heart. . . . It's a problem of a heart that won't break and holds pain in defiance of a breaking point. It should break. In this world things are too poignant. I feel so boxed in, I fear my legs will collapse if I don't change my experience quick— either off or into the ground. Food changes the experience of where I'm at—NOW.

I'm learning other ways of getting beyond it—prayer and writing. When I am writing, I have no eating problem. Disciplined prayer is active listening. It can produce the third [the transcendent function] that can change things. It leads to a way out or at least a way of living in opposition. Art and prayer are closely related. Art is a bridge to the other world.

Sometimes I stand on a street-corner wondering what I am doing. I feel like two stencilled forms and I'm trying to get them together. One me can feel life; the other me carries me out of it all. My life is like the ending of a Chinese poem: "And stop after stop is the end of the road."

I think I cannot go on. The tide comes in. There's no meaning . . . there's no meaning . . . there's no meaning. The third time it goes right over me. I can't find my relationship to God and all the world recedes. All meaning suddenly drains out of life. That's the perilousness of it. I just never know. After each stop is a new beginning. Everything is telescoped down to this hour. I live morning, then afternoon, then evening.

I have quoted from discussions with Anne at length because her articulation of her inner world gives us such a searing insight into the anguish of the anorexic adolescent. Her motivations, her complexes, and conflicts are very like those of Margaret, and like those of any other woman in whom body and spirit are seriously split.

Both girls have idealized father-images—Margaret because she rejected her father and projected her masculinity onto an Old Testament Jehovah; Anne, because she saw her father in festive situations and projected her "real" father onto "an emperor" who scrutinized the dignity with which she accepted punishment from his surrogates. Both were princesses of whom much was required by their mothers who were also worshipping a tyrannical father-image—a tyrant who loved so long as he was obeyed, and rejected as soon as he was crossed.

Because neither mother was conscious of her own femininity, she was unable to give her daughter an instinctual love of her own body, and thus the feminine ego was split off from the feminine spirit locked in her own earth. The terrible sense of being "caged" and longing to smash out is the energy of that rejected feminine pounding on her prison bars, demanding release. As children their energy was naturally directed into learning, but the pressure to be outstanding created a compulsive desire for books, for clarity, for exactness; the oversensitive little girl who needed to cry and be cuddled was left to pine in her body prison. The fantasy world with the father grew into insatiable longing for perfection and truth, reinforced by her hostility to all that was "obscure, instinctive, ambiguous, and unconscious in her own nature."[78] Although she may have felt close to her mother, mother and daughter were both victims of a negative mother complex, and both threatened by the hell of the "chaos of the maternal womb."[79]

The Great Goddess has to be acknowledged at first menstruation. Without a mother who can instinctively give her a deep reverence for this mystery, reverence for the childbirth associated with it, and reverence for her own body as the instrument through which Life incarnates, the daughter reacts with terror. This terror is in proportion to the nature and intensity of her father complex, which will be discussed more fully in Chapter IV. Sufficient to say here that her flight from the feminine drives her off the ground into a craving for perfection, order, and what Shelley called "the white radiance of Eternity."[80] This inflation is compensated by the feminine, which rebels against the air and violently swings back to concrete earth, nature, life, food. The unthinkable sexual fantasies are also displaced onto food, and for a religious girl, the complex is further charged by desire for union with God as an escape from a world with which she cannot cope.

Anne's childhood behaviour was somewhat at variance with the sweet, compliant, considerate attitude of most anorexics. She was something of a rebel from the beginning because of her artistic creativity. She was concerned with "doing everything right and fitting in," but her sense of fun and her honesty burst through that desire and made her seem rebellious. However, the real fire of her rebellion and the uniqueness of her personality she kept hidden, because she "would have alienated everyone." "I was too honest," she said. "I would have made life too hard for myself." When the anorexia did burst out, the full-fledged rebel burst with it.

In *The Golden Cage*, Hilde Bruch emphasizes that among the members of the anorexic girl's family there is usually a "clinging attachment and a peculiarly intense sharing of ideas and feelings," but the child is not "acknowledged as an individual in her own right."[81] It may be worth considering here that a highly intuitive, highly intelligent child, who has been raised in close intimacy with the parents, may be hypersensitive to all that is going on unconsciously in and out of the home. She may, in fact, be carrying the shadow in almost every situation she enters. If she voices what she feels, she becomes a threat to everyone, so that she begins to experience herself as a Cassandra. She learns to keep her mouth shut and articulates her thoughts through her pen in secret. The real personality is in the writing. This may lead to salvation or destruction.

Her natural bent is towards perfection, purification, aesthetics. Her ideal is to remove all the superficial veils until only essence is left. If she fasts, she quickly experiences her hypersensitivity to each of her five senses, and her hyperacuity to her own unconscious. Once she experiences the intensity of fasting and the power in herself which that releases, she may find it "rich to die/ To cease upon a midnight with no pain."[82] For her, this is no longer a negation of life, but an active desire for the perfection of death. Any art form—writing, music, dance—may become the "deceiving elf" that beckons her. On the other hand, art may be essential to her as a mediator between the two worlds. Being able to express her feelings in some concrete way, especially through creative dance, may help her to contact her own inner life spirit, and help her to feel she has a home on this earth and wants to stay a while.

Whereas the obese girl is unable to outwit nature, the anorexic feels she succeeds. It would seem that the demonic life force drives the one deeper into the earth, whereas the other is propelled into

Common Factors

1. Clinging dependency in family group, but child not loved for her individuality.
2. Rigid control in the home.
3. Basic disturbance in self-awareness and body awareness.
4. Inability to recognize hunger and other body sensations.
5. Repressed emotions, too compliant, too desirous to fulfil parents' unlived lives.
6. Food problems probably began at onset of menstruation.
7. Infantile attitude towards sexuality.
8. Unaware of her own feelings and feminine needs, therefore unable to live her own life.
9. Attempt to gain control over her own life through eating or refusing to eat.
10. Believes cultural fantasy that thinness will solve her problems.
11. Weak ego. Basic self-deception. Danger of psychotic break.
12. Haunted by parents' projections. Desire to be perfect counterbalanced by sense of inner worthlessness.
13. Food problem related to religious problem and demonic animus.
14. Death wish compensated by fierce desire for life.
15. Overwhelming sense of aloneness.

Contrasting Factors

Obese	*Anorexic*
1. Terror of being fat equals terror of deprivation.	1. Terror of being fat.
2. Tends to remain outwardly compliant in teens.	2. Tends to become rebellious and stubborn.
3. Considers herself ugly, cowardly failure in eyes of parents and peer group.	3. Feels acceptable in culture. Wins admiration through losing weight at first.
4. Develops sense of moral inferiority.	4. Happy in moral strength to stay with diet.
5. Cyclic starvation, binging.	5. Cyclic starvation, binging, ritual vomiting.
6. Refuses to put fantasies to the test; believes everything could still be right if she were thin.	6. Attempts to put fantasies to the test by dieting.
7. Preoccupation with Darkness.	7. Preoccupation with Light.

Table 4. Some comparisons between neurotically obese and anorexic girls.

the air, Darkness as opposed to Light—but both away from life. Because the anorexic girl's life is at stake, she is forced to look at her fantasies in terms of reality, or to become schizophrenic, or to die. The obese girl's inability to follow her diet allows her to hold onto her fantasies and thus avoid the recognition of her failure to face reality. By holding onto them, she fails to find the core of her personality at the cost of her own self-respect. She is in danger of masking her unspoken despair, her pervading sense of helplessness and hopelessness. As we saw in Chapter II, that Darkness has pathological results—physiologically and psychologically—which may manifest when she comes to menopause and feels she has missed her feminine life.

Some comparisons between obese and anorexic girls are given in Table 4, page 81.

KATHERINE (48 years, 5'9", 165 pounds)

Katherine's serpent dream was presented in Chapter II to illustrate the power of the life force cut off from the main flow of energy in her body. Her material illustrates what can happen in middle age when conflicts such as those experienced by Margaret and Anne are not dealt with in adolescence. Katherine believed that will-power could end her weight problem, but she learned that diet is only surgery that ultimately fails unless the root of the symptom is removed. Her father had been obese, and although she had freed herself from his physical proportions when she dieted, she had not broken her psychic relationship to him, nor had she found her own femininity. As she approached the second half of life, the Self demanded that she find her own totality. Thus she had to recognize that nature and spirit have their own laws to which the ego must eventually bow.

She belongs to the primarily obese because all the members of her family were big people, she was a ten-pound baby, and fat until she was twenty-one. Then she decided her scholarly world was not enough. She dieted and danced her way to a slim 125 pounds, only to find three years later that her body was retaining water and putting on weight in spite of dieting. At thirty-two, after a series of blackouts, her condition was diagnosed as cyclic edema. For twenty years, she maintained the weight and water under rigid control between 150-170 pounds.

Cyclic edema is a harrowing symptom if a woman is trying to maintain her weight by overactivity and rigid diet. She awakes one morning, her face puffed, her eyes swollen shut, and her body painfully distended. She cannot understand what happened. If her doctor does not recognize the symptom, he smiles and tells her that she didn't put that on by eating air. Her reaction is inner panic, partly psychological, partly physical, because the pressure in her body is unendurable. (A twenty-two year old in this study, after such an interview, actually took a razor blade to her stomach in an effort to release the pressure.) If she becomes accustomed to the symptom, she can relax into it. She is drugged. She moves like a sleepwalker. She smiles and speaks, but she isn't there. Nothing can touch her.

In spite of the symptom, Katherine lived a very active, creative life. She married but had no children. During the prime years of her adulthood, she was able to push her body to extremes of exhaustion, at which time the edema became so heavy she was forced to sleep. When she relaxed, she dreamed, the water was released, and she returned to normal. Gradually, the periods of sleep increased to two to three days out of seven, at which point she entered analysis.

This was the crisis of her life. Von Franz speaks of such a turning point in the following passage:

> The whole life energy . . . was accumulating in the deeper layers of the unconscious, to come through with a shock. Nature has tried over and over to get through, but then seems to wait until it has accumulated a great charge. But this is dangerous, because then she comes in a dangerous form, so . . . you may come to a shock solution, or a shock catastrophe, for nature does not care which. Realization may only come on the death-bed, and in the end there may be a cancer, and realization may happen in the last hour. There has been a quiet period when nature has been accumulating . . . . the mother complex has taken on the form of a destructive dragon. Because there is no fight with it (they just walk past it), this means the devouring mother has now taken on her deepest, coldest and most destructive form, and has disappeared into the bowels of the earth. Nothing happens above any more. If an archetype takes on the form of a snake or a dragon, it is in such deep layers that it manifests only in the sympathetic nervous system, and the conflict is in such a form that it cannot be assimilated. There will not even be any more important dreams. It is the stillness before the storm.[83]

Katherine was fortunate in that she did enter analysis, and she was able to contact her snake. Thinking of her inner world, she wrote in her journal:

When I feel light and happy and in love with life, I feel I am only out
of prison for a little while and I will have to return. I begin to feel
guilty. I know the suffering will return. I fall into hopelessness and feel
my body filling with water. The pressure grows until I move in a trance
in order to keep moving at all. Then the trance leads me to the bigger
water. My God, that's Ophelia! And for the same reason! She betrayed
Hamlet because she could not disobey her father. Is the demon I try to
escape the jealous, ruthless Jehovah that my father worshipped?

The real dragon in me lies in the water. It lies in a dark lagoon in the
depths of my Being. It is repressed feeling and femininity—the best part
of myself turned into a pestilent pool so strenuously dammed back. My
lovely feminine waters—my natural love, my joy, my anger, my grief in
all the innuendoes of the intensity with which I experience them—all
rarely expressed. Fear is the dam—fear of rejection, fear of rejection from
the men I love most.

Old Mother Alchemy with her dropsy was unconscious in her lower
parts, unconscious of her living feminine feeling. I tried to tell myself
just to get on with life, make the most of it, fat or thin. No use crying.
C'est la vie. But then a voice said, "You have no right to hope. You
aren't like other women. You have no right to live." When the pain of all
that became too great, I sank into the sea of my own unshed tears.

But drowning as I was, I was also clinging to something in those
waters. I relaxed into unconsciousness, gave up the ego, and trusted in
another voice. I ceased to worry and I ceased to fight. I simply went
where I was taken through dangers that would have been death if my
eyes had been open. Is this, in fact, an experience of the dark side of the
Self, paradoxically destroying me and saving me at the same time? Is it
my fear of that overwhelming power that makes me experience it as a
demon until I relax into it? I thought I had conquered the dark god
when I refused to get lost in fat. But now my ego strength only sucks me
deeper. Perhaps if I were consciously being led, I would not be afraid.
Perhaps my real feelings could find natural expression. Then I could
free the Holy Spirit that is drowned in those waters. Then I could surrender to a loving God and be truly baptised. I could accept the unknown—even if it means accepting homelessness for home.

Katherine's dreams helped her to reconnect to her lost feminine.
Over a period of months, through dreams and active imagination,
her wise old gypsy woman initiated her into the feminine rites, made
her conscious of her own instinctual wisdom and her own receptive
nature. Gradually, she learned to keep in contact with her real feelings and to express them in spontaneous situations. Contact with
her feminine nature made her less fearful of rejection. Her dependence on diuretics decreased; her edemic episodes were more rare
and less severe. She still had difficulty surrendering her ego, still
tended towards compulsive action, and tended to fear the chthonic

feminine. Then she had the following dream:

> My friend and I are swimming across a small lake. Suddenly I am frightened. We are too far out for me. He says, "Don't worry. Just don't fight and I'll take you to the other side." Then he draws a shape on the water, showing me that the opposites can be joined ⌣ rather than ⌢ . "Don't lose hold of the dark god now," he says. "The transcendent can come from the dark rather than the light. Your lacuna is in your dark god."

Her sudden loss of confidence, her fear of being swallowed by the water, her fear of trusting her own animus—all are clear in the initial situation. That fear drove her away from Being into compulsive action. Her animus tells her not to struggle against him, but to relax and let things happen. The opposites can only be joined by holding both sides and allowing the dark god to come through the lacuna or small lake of her shadow side. Her real healing can come through nature.

For some weeks, she dreamed of black pools that she should jump into. Fear held her back. Then came the following dream:

> I was walking in darkness when I came upon a round jet-black area in the ground. It looked like the crater of a volcano, but I was not sure it was dead, nor what I might stir up if I jumped in. It was heavy, foul, mud. Then came a voice, more like a plea than a command, "Throw yourself into the abyss." I walked up to the brink and voices echoed all around me, "Trust—Trust—Trust . . . ." I jumped into the centre and as I fell I saw at the bottom of the abyss two golden S's joining together to make a figure 8, an infinity symbol. I landed in the middle. Instantly it turned vertically, one end burst into flame, and carried me to the top of the darkness.

Associating to this dream, Katherine said the abyss was parting with everything she knew. It was Death. Plunging through its darkness, she experienced her total aloneness and knew she was in a life-and-death struggle. The world became an illusion and the only reality was in the two golden S's, the Spiritus Sanctus, at the bottom of the hole. She thought of a text that went something like this: "The King's son lies in the depths of the sea as though dead. But he lives and calls from the deep, 'Whosoever will free me from the waters and lead me to dry land, him will I prosper with everlasting riches.'"[84] She said, "His was the voice calling to me from the slime. I thought I was rescuing Him and He rescued me."

In *Woman's Mysteries*, Esther Harding tells the myth of the moon sending a deluge upon the earth, but at the same time providing a means of salvation, a crescent moon-boat in which her people were carried to the sun, the place of warmth and light. Commenting on the myth she writes:

> Surely [the psychological meaning of this arc is] that redemption from the cold-blooded attitude of the unconscious waters of instinct, representing the dark of the moon, is to be found by gaining a different relation to the moon goddess. To be saved in the boat of the goddess is not the same thing as being engulfed by the waters of the moon. To climb into her boat means to become one of her company. It is a religious symbol. . . . The salvation is to be found by taking a new attitude towards the power of instinct, involving the recognition that it is, in itself, not human, but belongs to the nonhuman or divine realm. To enter the boat of the goddess implies accepting the uprush of instinct in a religious spirit as a manifestation of the creative life force itself. When such an attitude is attained, instinct can no longer be regarded as an asset to be exploited for the advantage of the personal life, instead it must be recognized that the personal I, the ego, must submit itself to the demands of the life force as to a divine being.[85]

Having overcome her terror of the chthonic feminine and her desire to hold onto the conscious ego position, Katherine surrendered to what she felt could be death. But in that death she found the life force imprisoned in the waters and the Holy Spirit carried her in a burst of living flame towards the sun. Her Spiritus Sanctus, which had been buried in the muddy water, was suddenly transformed by her act of trust into a symbol of the timelessness of the soul which acted as an arc to carry her toward consciousness. Her dark god came through the lacuna and helped her to transcend her impasse.

Katherine realized that her drivenness and depression were attributable to tremendous inner drives which were not being carried out. These were repressed by resignation which constituted the nucleus of the depression in the unconscious. Again, to quote von Franz:

> That is why when you get people out of such a state they first turn into a hungry lion which wants to eat up everything, the depression having been only a compensation, or repression mechanism, because they do not know how to cope with this tremendous drive.[86]

Up to this point, Katherine had never had the courage to draw on her own creative depths. Much of her libido was locked in her unconscious, leaving depression in consciousness.

What did Katherine's symptom symbolize? Clearly, the Self was bending her ego to its preappointed plan, using her body as its medium. Through ego-strength she became slender, but her ego was powerless against the new symptom which looked like the hated fat.

Her attempts to escape from her feelings only locked them in the tears which she carried on her hips and thighs. Her conventional life had become a prison, whose narrow confines she sought to forget by running faster on her treadmill; her intense emotions she sought to ignore and in so doing handed over her personal fate to blind nature.

Fortunately for her, nature was not blind. Physiologically, cyclic edema may be likened to an allergy. When too much "poison" enters the body, the body retains water to anaesthetize and protect itself from too much pain.[87] It defends its own particular chemistry from invasion by too many foreign elements. Her too empathetic nature left Katherine vulnerable to too many psychic invaders. Thus instinct was protecting her and showing her how to protect herself. Periodically, she was forced into her feminine waters, forced to succumb to her own inner rhythms. The archetypal situation appeared in her dream images as a fish, musing silently in her own unconscious depths, feeding on the fantasies and dreams which could bring new life to her body and to her ego. In that timeless world at the bottom of the sea, she was free from schedules and conflicts and pain. So long as her ego was not strong enough to handle the tension, the pain moved into her body, and the edema allowed her to regress into the protection of the womb which at that time she required.[88] At the same time, it acted as body armour against further attack.

When she was able to listen to her body and recognize its messages in consciousness, the edema gradually abated. Gradually, through amplifications, she was able to accept these waters as divine, part of the feminine cycle of the waxing and waning of the moon. Gradually she realized that the flooding was sometimes part of a "creative depression," a pregnancy, forerunner to the creative outbursts which were essential to her life. Her creativity depended on the gentle, constant flow of feeling; otherwise, she was exhausted by the rigidity of trying too hard and accomplishing very little.

In *Mysterium Coniunctionis,* Jung wrote at length concerning the transformation of the old king through water.[89] In brief, the parable is as follows. When he was about to enter battle, the king asked his servant to bring him water. "I demand the water which is closest to my heart, and which likes me above all things." Then he drank so much that "all his limbs were filled and all his veins inflated, and he himself became discoloured." His soldiers put him into a heated chamber to sweat the water out, but when they opened the door, "he lay there as if dead." Egyptian physicians tore him into little pieces, ground them to powder, mixed them with medicines and put him back in the chamber. When he was brought out he was half dead. Alexandrian physicians ground the body a second time, washed it and dried it, added new substances and placed it in a crucible-shaped chamber with holes bored in the bottom. After an hour they heaped fire upon it and melted it so that the liquid ran into the vessel below. Then the king rose up from death and shouted, "Where are my enemies? I shall kill them all if they do not submit to me."

Commenting on this parable, Jung wrote:

> The idea was to extract the pneuma or psyche . . . . from matter . . . . in the form of a volatile or liquid substance, and thereby to mortify the "body." This *aqua permanens* was then used to revive or reanimate the "dead" body, and paradoxically, to extract the soul again. The old body has to die; it was either sacrificed or simply killed, just as the old king had either to die or to offer sacrifice to the gods.[90]

The Self demanded such a dissolution of Katherine in order to purify her ego, and bring her to surrendering to the Holy Spirit. Only then could the god in her Darkness ignite, thus re-animating her "dead" body and freeing her soul.

Turning the spotlight into the hearts of these three women reveals the hidden anguish of the buried feminine soul. Margaret and Anne were in the first half of life striving for ego formation; Katherine was in the second half when, in the process of individuation, the ego had to surrender to the Self. Fatness, studied as a symptom, can no longer be considered merely an inflation, nor an attempt to retain everything, nor a desire for power feeding a greedy animus. Nor is overeating simply an attempt to punish oneself and others, especially mother who never gave enough. The focussed light reveals how perfectly the arrow fits the wound. "The wounding and painful shafts do not come from outside . . . but from the ambush of our own unconscious. It is our own repressed desires that stick like arrows in our flesh."[91]

CHAPTER IV

LOSS OF THE FEMININE

> The Maenads . . . are the frenzied sanctified
> women who are devoted to the worship of
> Dionysus. But they are something more:
> they tend the god as well as suffer his
> inspiration.
>
> —*The Notebooks of Martha Graham*

Obesity is one of the chief symptoms of neurosis in the Western world. The millions of dollars spent on research, diets, and exercise spas attest to the futility of our efforts to cope with it.[92] Thinness has become a mania tending to focus the neurosis on food, but the roots of the problem remain diseased. Many thousands of anorexic girls, starving and running themselves to collapse, are denying the traditional female role, preferring to regress into childhood. Many thousands of their fat sisters are in the equally agonizing throes of a slow process of destruction. Both are in a blood pact with Death.

Blaming the parents is a convenient dismissal of this cultural enormity. These girls speak of their weight with the same embarrassment that women once spoke of their sexual lives.[93] Is it possible that the repressed god that was somatised as hysteria in the early part of this century is now appearing in obesity and anorexia nervosa?

The twenty obese volunteers in this study belong to the 40% of overweight American women and are very much a product of the Western way of life. A more detailed analysis of the significant complexes revealed through the Association Experiment shows how the individual problem is mirroring a cultural pattern.

89

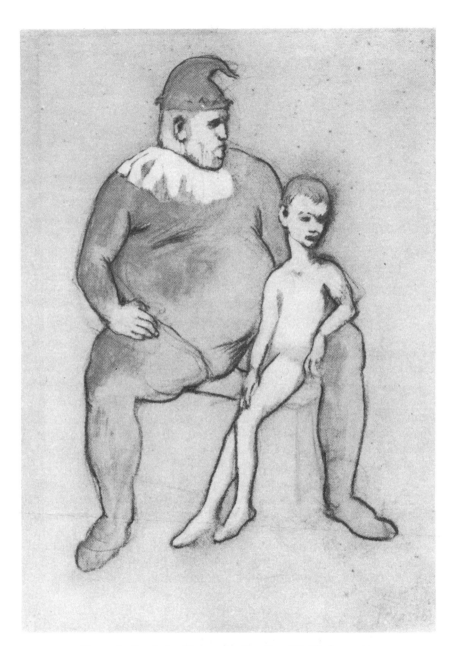

Figure 3. Study by Picasso for *Family of Saltimbanques*.
(Baltimore Museum of Art, Cone Collection)

The Father Complex

Of the twenty obese women, twelve had positive father complexes and eight had idealized their absent or alcoholic fathers. Among the controls, twelve had positive father complexes and two idealized fathers, but fifteen of the controls also had positive mothers, whereas the obese had only four. The positive father, without the positive mother, may take on the maternal characteristics as well. In the three cases discussed in Chapter III, two had alcoholic fathers and compensated with intense projections on an idealized father-god; the third had a positive father complex with equally intense projections on a father-god. As far as I could discern, the fathers were all puers. It is that peculiarly intimate sharing of ideas and feelings with the father which seems to be a decisive factor in the psyche of the obese woman.

The accompanying Picasso print (Figure 3, opposite) vividly illustrates the split in the daughter's animus. Part of her is drawn to the delicate puer, the romantic dreamer, the blue-haired idealist who longs to escape from life's realities in his search for a better world. Towards him, her feelings are split. Part of her is the puella who shares his characteristics and shares his search for spiritual meaning; part of her is mother whose sole desire is to nourish her boy and protect him from pain.

Because the father in most cases is a "mother's son," he has a close contact with his own unconscious, cherishing those creative depths which he seeks to share with an inspiratrice. He needs his daughter to fulfil that role, acting as a bridge to the unconscious; he needs her also to be mother acting as buffer between him and reality. The fat clown is the other side of the puer, the senex.[94] Positively, he is the wise old man who respects order, stability, and security, and conducts his life responsibly and with authority. Negatively he is a Saturn figure, with the astrological qualities of that planet: "drivenness, creative depression and despair, heaviness, suffering, imprisonment, helplessness, dehumanization."[95]

Because the two sides of the archetype are not integrated in her father, the girl is "bewitched" by his unconscious. Thus she carries his heaviness and his clown's sense of tragedy and irony. At her happiest dance, she hears the echoing "Vanity, vanity, all is vanity" and feels her feet become lead beneath her. Because her Logos model is lacking in stability and inner authority, she also lacks the resources to fight the depression with order and light. As a quaternity, the relationship between father and daughter might be sketched as in Figure 4.[96]

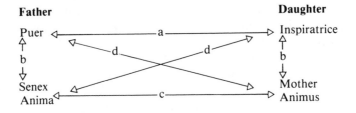

Figure 4. Psychological dynamics of father-daughter relationship.

Several relationships are evident and these will merge into each other:
a) The personal relationship.
b) The relationship of each to the unconscious.
c) The relationship of animus and anima with shadow complications.
d) The relationship of the daughter's animus to her father, and the relationship of the father's anima to the daughter.

The unconscious situation is apparent from the diagram. The mother (matter, body) is linked unconsciously with the senex and all his Saturnine heaviness. Perhaps the combination of these two archetypes lies behind the prematurely maternal figure of the obese girl.

If there was parental discord and if her father in his disappointment turned his anima projection onto his daughter, unconsciously she became his child-bride, raped before her time. But to that husband she may remain true for the rest of her life, whether in her choice of husband, or her inability to marry, or her inability to bring Eros into sexuality. Unconsciously, she may be caught in an incestuous marriage. (In Freudian terms, she has an Electra complex). Unless she recognizes that her father-lover is her own inner ideal man who must not be projected onto a human man, she may spend her life searching for her ghostly lover. If she finds her "ideal," she may be bound for double-edged tragedy because the golden arrows will probably strike a puer searching for a mother-bride. Their marriage would then be double incest.

Behind the father complex is the archetype of God the Father. The puella who adores or idealizes her puer father will look to this God for light and justice, though unconsciously she may fear His treachery. Consciously she seeks beauty and truth; unconsciously the dark forces in her puer animus rebel against a just Jehovah and unwittingly she may ally herself with Lucifer. Literature is full of such "innocent maidens."

In "Eloa," a poem by Vigny, the Devil's sweetheart is an angel who never came to Earth. She was a daughter of Christ, sprung from a tear shed by Jesus over the tomb of Lazarus. Her mission was to console the afflicted. She is the celestial archetype of those mortal women who give their lives to suffering men, hoping to raise and redeem them. Not happy in Heaven with her brother angels, she yearned to descend into Hell to console her condemned brothers because they needed her. The angel most in need of her sympathy was Lucifer himself. One day she encountered an angel of surpassing beauty and seductive eloquence. Unaware of his identity, the naive maiden was seduced by his tears and fatal charm. Her pity changed into love. Wrapped in a cloud, the two passed together to Hell but their dialogue was overheard by a chorus of cherubim:

> Où me conduisez-vous, bel ange? —Viens toujours.
> —Que votre voix est triste, et quel sombre discours!
> N'est-ce pas Eloa qui soulève ta chaine?
> J'ai cru t'avoir sauvé.—Non, c'est moi qui t'entraîne.
> Si nous sommes unis, peu m'importe en quel lieu!
> Nomme-moi donc encore ou ta Soeur ou ton Dieu!
> —J'enlève mon esclave et je tiens ma victime.
> —Tu paraissais si bon! Oh! qu'ai je fait? —Un crime.
> —Seras-tu plus heureux? du moins, est-tu content?
> —Plus triste que jamais. —Qui donc es-tu? —Satan.[97]

Seduced by his loneliness and her own pity, Eloa wistfully asks in the last two lines if he will not be happy, at least content. Then comes the answer she must have feared: "More sad than ever." "Who are you?" she asks. "Satan," he replies.

Eloa personifies that sweet maid who swings between taking responsibility for the Devil himself and taking no responsibility at all. Her conscious dedication to noble purposes leaves her unconscious demon to constellate in her partner, who may live out her shadow animus. She fails to become a human woman who can look herself straight in the eye and accept her limitations and her strength. Her

father's "perfection" has made her expect too much of herself and
too much of others. Jehovah is always standing in judgement over
her and she must do all in her power to please Him, even at the cost
of her own integrity. Relationship to her man is all-important. "He
for God only and she for God in him."[98] Unless she is very secure
in herself, such a woman will sacrifice even her own feelings in order
to maintain the one relationship that holds her in life. If she betrays
her own feeling depths, she falls into the arms of her negative animus
who may become destructive enough to kill her. Her devotion to
the Apollinian order of life, coupled with her fear of the demon,
drives her to seek ego control through animus activity. In ignoring
her puella side, however, she is forfeiting her connection to Dionysus,
thus forfeiting the essential component of her female nature.

Eloa, as part of a Christian myth, makes an interesting contrast
to the Greek Persephone. Both were innocent maidens seduced by
the god of the Underworld. Persephone, however, was firmly rooted
on the earth in her close relationship to her mother; thus, she was
able to give herself to Hades and at the appointed time to bring forth
their son, Dionysus, whose cradle, a winnowing basket containing a
single ear of grain, was the most venerated object at the great har-
vest festival celebrated at Eleusis.

Eloa, on the other hand, has no human mother and no human
body, and is therefore unrelated to reality. Her life is sprung from a
sentimental, masculine tear which pities mortals for their human lot.
Such sentimentality rejects the realities of living on Earth. Eloa,
blinding herself to her own evil, and inflated by her own desire to
save, is at the same time unconsciously rebelling against a god who
allows evil. She consequently becomes vulnerable to Satan, the arch-
rebel. Without close kinship to Mother Demeter, she lacks firm roots
in her own sexuality. She has no ground with which to deal with the
shadow and may become a purposeless martyr to the man she sets
out to save. Neither Dionysus nor a living Christ can be born without her body.

The modern Eloa refuses to be the victim of the man or God she
once adored. However, because she is still not taking responsibility
for her own devil, she tends to project him onto the masculine world,
where she seeks revenge for the murder of her femininity. Bewitched
by her own masculine power drive and unconnected to her own
Demeter, she fails to see in her revenge a disguised form of self-
murder. This makes the passover to sacrifice impossible. Her lost
femininity is neither rediscovered nor redeemed.

The Mother Complex

Where a woman is possessed by an eating disorder, even more crucial than the father complex is the mother. The confusion of instincts probably goes back to earliest infancy. A baby has a different
cry for different needs, but the mother who cannot interpret those
cries, or hasn't the inner resources to respond in differentiated ways,
or hasn't the love to fulfil them, answers every cry with food. And
when the baby is stuffed, she wonders why it vomits. How could it
be so ungrateful? Speaking of the child's later problems, Hilde
Bruch writes:

> Inability to identify bodily sensations correctly is a specific disability
> in eating disorders; other feeling tones, too, are inaccurately perceived
> or conceptualized, and often associated with the inability to recognize
> the implications of interactions with others.[99]

The mother who is out of touch with her own body cannot give her
baby the sense of harmony with the Self and the universe which is
fundamental to her later sense of totality.

Erich Neumann discusses the importance of the positive contact
provided by the primal relationship in *The Child*:

> The order and morality of the Great Mother are conditioned by the
> child's experience of the order of its own body and of the cosmic
> rhythm of day and night and of the seasons. This rhythm determines
> the life of the entire organic world and the main rituals of mankind
> are attuned to it . . . Through the harmony between the child's own
> rhythm and that of the mother—who in the primal relationship is ex-
> perienced as identical with its own—the mother's image becomes the
> representative of both the inner and outer world . . . . The root of
> the earliest and most basic matriarchal morality is then to be sought
> in a harmony between the still unsplit total personality of the child
> and the Self which is experienced through the mother.[100]

Neumann goes on to point out that where the primal relationship is
disturbed, the child blames itself, and being unloved becomes synonymous with being abnormal, guilty, alone. Later, a girl's own Self
becomes the Terrible Mother, whose rejection denies her child the
right to live. Because the child experiences the animus of the mother
as hostile, a paradox develops. It comes to experience any higher
ordering principle as an assault on its psyche. The psyche reacts with
fear, but the fear is the fear of chaos.

If the primal relationship is positive, then the child can accept the
assault of the higher ordering principle because the predominance

of the Eros principle gives it the courage to accept the negative over-
powering. It can die and know it will be reborn. If the primal relationship is negative, however, the frightened ego, to which the instinct of self-preservation has prematurely given rise, substitutes aggression and defence mechanisms for the security that the negative
mother was unable to give.[101]

In a society where so many mothers have lost touch with the
rhythm of their own natures, it is not surprising that the fear of life
is fundamental in so many personalities. The child who is not allowed
to live her own spontaneous rhythms develops a petrifying fear of
the power of her own instincts because she is cut off from her own
inner Being, and therefore cut off from the reality of life.

Such a child becomes an adult woman who simply does not com-
prehend the feminine principle. For her, "being receptive" means
surrendering control, opening herself to Fate, and plummeting
through chaotic darkness into an abyss that has no bottom. No loving arms will open to receive her as she falls. Therefore she dare not
surrender to Life—the consequences could be fatal. Even if the door
of her cage stood open, she could not dare to walk through. If she
acted out of her own instincts and voiced her own feelings, she
would make herself vulnerable to what Fate has to offer. Better to
try to keep control by remaining silent and acting out the roles of
daughter, wife, and mother as she has always half-heartedly understood them.

Indeed, she may be making the only choice she can. To yield to
the Great Goddess is to accept life as it is: winter today, spring tomorrow; cruelty juxtaposed with beauty, aloneness following love.
Yielding is possible only when one knows the arms of the loving
mother—or perhaps the outstretched wings of the Holy Ghost—are
open to enfold the falling child. In the fateful crises, one may really
have no choice.

The obese woman is living out a double bind. Her obsession with
weight protects her from the conscious confrontation with the opposites—a confrontation which is the only way to the wholeness
for which she longs. As a woman, her feminine instinct tells her she
must yield, but she is terrified of losing the control which, in fact,
she does not have. At the same time she knows she dare not yield,
for fear her worst terrors will be realized: the arms of love are not
there. Nor can a loving man be both lover and surrogate mother.
Her healing must come through the abyss of the absent feminine.

never step out of this mill—this awful, grinding, banal life in which they are "nothing but." In the ritual they are near the Godhead; they are even divine.[104]

The woman who has lost her role as one of the actors in the divine drama of life feels herself out of "the lap of the All-compassionate Mother."[105] That thing in her which should live is alone; nobody touches it, nobody knows it, she herself doesn't know it; but it keeps on stirring, it disturbs her, it makes her restless, and it gives her no peace. In response to a rabbi's intellectual granddaughter, a woman who was experiencing abysmal fear, Jung said:

> You have been untrue to your God. . . . You have forsaken the mystery of your race. You belong to holy people, and what do you live? No wonder that you fear God, that you suffer from the fear of God.[106]

This fear is in many modern women; in fact, it is at the root of the fanatic side of the Feminist Movement in America. Mary Daly, one of the most outspoken feminists, fiercely rejected her Roman Catholicism with its tyrant Jehovah. In *Beyond God the Father,* her attack on "patriarchal space" is vitriolic:

> The appearance of change is basically only separation and return— cyclic movement. Breaking out of the circle requires anger, the "wrath of God" speaking God-self in an organic surge toward life. Since women are dealing with demonic power relationships, that is, with structured evil, rage is required as a positive creative force, making possible a break-through, encountering the blockages of inauthentic structures. It rises as a reaction to the shock of recognizing what has been lost—before it had ever been discovered—one's own identity. Out of this shock can come intimations of what human being (as opposed to half being) can be. Anger, then, can trigger and sustain movement from the experience of nothingness to recognition of participation in being. . . . When women take positive steps to move out of patriarchal space and time, there is a surge of new life.[107]

Her very bitterness suggests some deep personal rage, some overwhelming personal fear, some brutal disinheritance from her own feminine nature.

This same restless longing appeared repeatedly in the statements of women in the experiment. "I know if I were right with God, I would be right with my body." "I cannot grow in the life of the spirit until I grow to love my body." The inner connection between religious and physical food is obvious. What they long for is "their daily bread," but they take the symbol concretely. Each one believes that physical thinness can somehow lead to spiritual fatness. What they fail to realize is that there is a spirit which longs to be incarnated in their bodies, and that relationship to that spirit can bring them to an awareness of their own feminine Being. Only when they surrender to that spirit will their body reflect that totality.

Instead of seeking the spirit outside, they must learn to hear the voice of their own abandoned Self, and thus reconnect with their own inner mystery. Only by that route can they come to the feeling of belonging to life and sense the reality for which they yearn.

This confusion of spirit and body is quite understandable in a culture where spirit is concretized in magnificent skyscrapers, where cathedrals have become museums for tourists, where woman-flesh-devil are associated, and nature is raped for any deplorable excuse. It is even more understandable if we think of the child growing up in suburbia, seeing her father only on weekends, when he brings the treats, while the week is spent with the disciplinarian mother. It also follows that, in this unconscious confusion of masculinity and femininity, the young girl would see in her unrelated, bloated body, the dark side of a god who had turned against her. The more she fights him, the more she is consumed by him, and the greater her fear of annihilation. Dieting with fierce will-power is the masculine route; dieting with love of her own nature is the feminine. Her only real hope is to care for her own body and experience it as the vessel through which her Self may be born.

The great danger for the obese woman is the displacement of one instinct onto another. The joy of Eros in the bedroom is forfeited for the greed of Hecate in the kitchen. The sexual longing for wholeness is redirected into food, and the ecstasy of eating takes on the emotional connotations of sexuality and religion. Eating until the ego slips into the unconscious becomes a parody of orgasm; behind it is the longing for release of tension in peace, sleep, or even death.

The woman who has not found herself in her own body is dependent on a man to help her to be born on this earth, and is therefore inclined to project her Self onto the man she loves. Sexuality then becomes overendowed with spiritual overtones. When faith and love are synonymous, she will project God onto her man, only to witness the collapse of that bridge not constructed to bear such weight. By whatever route, she must find her own God within.

Conclusion

How are these five complexes interrelated? All have one thing in common—the loss of the feminine ego. Virginia Woolf once wrote that women are condemned by society to function as mirrors, reflecting men at twice their actual size. This situation has somewhat changed, but the fact still remains that most women do not know how to be feminine except in relation to a man. As Jung pointed out:

> As long as a woman is content to be a *femme à homme* she has no feminine individuality. She is empty and merely glitters—a welcome vessel for masculine projections. Woman as a personality, however, is a different story: here illusion no longer works.[108]

The sad question arises, "What does a woman without her femininity see in the face of a similar woman? What does such a daughter see in the face of such a mother?" Surely, the only thing she can see is rejection, combined perhaps with a subtle defiance or cynicism. Very often this chasm is reinforced by the father's unconscious denigration of all that is essentially feminine. Thus the girl takes on an unconscious sense of guilt for being what she is. Her self-abnegation may lead her to try to find fulfilment in the masculine world, and at the same time to be a servant to all the men in her life. The sheer joy of being "I AM" she does not know, nor can she find it with other women.

The feminine mysteries of older cultures established an eternal bond between women—a bond that made them proud to be part of the life-stream that flowed through them. This bond, or its modern equivalent, conscious women in our culture are now seeking to re-establish.

CHAPTER V

REDISCOVERY OF THE FEMININE

> The dogma of the Assumption of Mary is in fact an acceptance of matter; indeed it is a sanctification of matter. If you were to analyse dreams, you would understand this better.
>
> —*C.G. Jung Speaking*

My study of obesity as a psychosomatic symptom in individual women led to the realization that obesity and anorexia nervosa are counterpoles of one neurosis. The further realization that governments are spending millions of dollars on research grants for both diseases, made me investigate the social implications more carefully.

In the Western countries threatened by these syndromes, the feminine has been devalued for centuries and is now profoundly distorted. In the individual suffering from these syndromes, the feminine is feared and rejected. Fat or thin, she is a woman of her time. Her rejected body epitomizes the present-day alienation from the feminine, and her obsession with her "daily bread" is only one cultural manifestation of the desperate search for spiritual meaning.

The way back to the feminine for the obese and the anorexic is no different from the way back for any woman. Society as a whole has to find the lost goddess. Jung has pointed out the importance of the dogma of the Assumption of the Virgin Mary as an acceptance of matter; indeed, in the lines quoted at the head of this chapter he says "it is a sanctification of matter." But what does it mean to experience our bodies as sacred? What does it mean to extract the psyche from matter and then to use that *aqua permanens* to reanimate the "dead" body and extract the soul again.[109] The answer may be rooted in our anatomy and, paradoxically, more mysterious than most of us realize.

102

The powerful Feminist Movements in the West are demanding recognition, but too often their approach is a mere parody of masculinity. Many thousands of women are taking up arms against patriarchal dominance; many others rejoice in the new rights for women which governments are being forced to recognize. Many others feel lost. They are appalled by the aggression of the militant Feminist leaders, but they recognize some profound emptiness in themselves. They try to be good wives and good mothers and good career women. But something is missing. They do not know how to be true to their own femininity. There is no feminine community to which they can relate; coffee-parties are no answer, nor is secret eating, nor secret drinking. If, however, these secretive acts are understood as a distorted instinctual drive towards wholeness, then the natural drive may be discovered behind the distortion.

Binges almost always comprise the ravenous eating of cereals, sweets, and milk products. Wheaten cakes and honey were the sacrificial food of Dionysus. Dipping the young animal in milk was part of the rite. Is the binge some archaic strata of the psyche demanding union with the gods and goddesses of the earth? This question brought me to a more careful study of the Dionysian Mysteries in the hope of understanding how the woman of previous cultures integrated her wild beast and allowed her own femininity to flower. This study brought me to a clearer understanding of the relationship between the Dionysian Mysteries and the "sanctification of matter" in the dogma of the Assumption. This relationship is the pivot of the discussion in this final chapter.

The Mystery Cult of Dionysus

The Dionysian "madness" inherent in compulsive eating may be a modern expression of what was earlier known as "possession" and in more recent years as "hysteria." As I have suggested, it may also be seen as a form of bewitchment. (Dionysus is said to have loathed the sight of an owl.) In our culture where the feminine is denigrated, where the ecstatic religious instincts springing from the body are felt to be perverse, and thinness at any price has become a god, nature takes her revenge. The repressed god whose needs are no longer recognized as prerequisites for psychic health demands recognition through somatic distortions. The god of nature ceases to be a spirit and possesses the woman as an autonomous animal. Fatness, not

sex, is a taboo in our culture, and fatness has taken on evil and
moral overtones. Reticence to speak of their actual weight was evident in the women who participated in the Association Experiment.
"Weight?" was a taboo question, almost always answered by "the
wrong side of 175," or some other euphemism.

Paradoxically, the woman yearning to be thin takes on the physical characteristics of Dionysus. This god was unique in that while
he was masculine, his followers were mostly women. Essentially, he
was androgynous—a bisexual god in whom male and female were
united.[110] If we look again at the complexes associated with compulsive eating and recognize the intensity of the "madness" involved, we can see the fierce masculine aggression combined with the
yearning feminine passivity, the desire for union in the peace of
wholeness. The symptom may be the cross on which thousands are
forced to writhe because they are unaware of the androgynous god
striving towards consciousness.

Nor can Dionysus be made conscious through the mind. The rational approach to obesity has proved futile for countless women.
Consciously they may understand why they are driven; unconsciously their actions resist change. The god demands recognition and,
willingly or unwillingly, they must pay their debt to him. Their
Greek and Roman counterparts, wives and mothers in an equally
patriarchal culture, surrendered to a Dionysian initiation in order
to find their feminine essence in relation to their own inner masculine spirit.

The Eleusinian Mysteries

In the Eleusinian Mysteries, the participants, in imitation of the
grieving goddess Demeter, fasted on their way to Eleusis, the place
of the finding of the Kore. The spiritual longing and lamentation
were not confused with personal physical hunger. Moreover, Persephone, in separating herself from her mother, was forbidden to
eat in the Underworld, but because she tasted of a pomegranate
while with Hades, she was never able totally to return to her mother.

The acceptance or rejection of food is symbolically crucial in all
religions. "To break bread" with the god is to be in communion
with him; to be hungry is to be alone, searching and preparing for
his advent through purification. The Maenads in the old Orphic
rites imitated the Titans in tearing apart Dionysus-Zagreus, as an

animal. Dionysus was both devoured and devourer, because while they tore apart his flesh, he was devouring them. But when a woman is able to participate in the "eating of the god" as a sacrifice transformed into a sacrament, then she no longer acts out of blind passion, because she consciously recognizes her own Titanic nature; then the god fills her with sacrificial food and thus releases her from her own savagery.

Only when the god is received into the stomach in this sacrificial way, can it be swallowed and incorporated into one's being. Bolting food is an animal ecstasy; an animal, however, cannot digest the meaning of the god. Because the Titans tore Dionysus to pieces, Zeus struck them with lightning, and from their ashes human beings were created. When the instinct is freed from its Titanic greed, then the *lykos*, the light of the soul, is free to seek its religious goal. The laurel twig which the Dionysian initiate carried symbolized her natural bent towards spiritual growth.

Demeter, as Great Earth Mother, conferred immortality on the son of the mythical king of Eleusis. As nurse to the infant Demophöon, she placed him each night in a manger of fire, thus transforming him into a divine child. Every woman who participated in the mysteries became a nurse to the child born in the depths of the Underworld. Immortality is one of Demeter's gifts and this immortality is akin to that of the grain:

> The grain figure is essentially the figure of both origin and end, of mother and daughter; and just because of that it points beyond the individual to the universal and eternal. It is always *the grain* that sinks to earth and returns, always the grain that is mown down in golden fullness and yet, as fat and healthy grain, remains whole, mother and daughter in one.[111]

During the rites, after the search and the sacred marriage, the torches shone, the "child" was presented, and the hierophant shouted, "The great goddess has borne a sacred child; Brimo has borne Brimos." (The Strong has brought forth Strength.) Kerényi points out that the child can only be her reborn daughter, but it is not the birth of a Kore that is proclaimed, but the birth of a divine boy. "Brimo is not Demeter *only*, as distinct from Persephone; she is non-differentiated mother and daughter. The child is likewise undifferentiated—it is only *what is born,* the fruit of birth."[112] A mown ear of grain was presented, *in silence,* and the participants were made aware of "the continuity of life in the unity of maiden, mother, and child, a being that dies, gives birth, and comes to life again."[113]

Demeter was identified with grain, the grain that never dies but grows up from the earth continually. Demeter is thus a biological image of the archetype of the Self. "The Self," wrote Jung,

> is a *borderline concept,* not by any means filled out with the known psychic processes. On the one hand it includes the phenomena of synchronicity, on the other its archetype is embedded in the brain structure and is physiologically verifiable: through electrical stimulation of a certain area of the brain-stem of an epileptic it is possible to produce mandala visions (*quadratura circuli*).[114]

Four is the double feminine and symbolizes the goal of the individuation process. Three is the masculine number and symbolizes the process itself. Three is also the number of Hecate and the Underworld.

Many modern women seem to have lost touch with the instinctual side of the psychoid archetype; it has fallen back into Hecate's cave. What was made known to the initiate at Eleusis is now rarely recognized as feminine consciousness. "The symbols of the Self," Jung wrote,

> arise in the depths of the body and they express its materiality every bit as much as the structure of the perceiving consciousness. The symbol is thus a living body, *corpus et anima*; hence the "child" is such an apt formula for the symbol.[115]

The words of a noble Abyssinian woman reveal how intrinsically related to the female body this archetypal image is:

> The woman is from the day of her first love another. That continues so all through life. The man spends a night by the woman and goes away. His life and body are always the same. The woman conceives. As a mother she is another person than the woman without child. She carries the fruit of the night for nine months in her body. Something grows. Something grows into her life that never again departs from it. She is a mother. She is and remains a mother even though her child die, though all her children die. For at one time she carried the child under her heart. And it does not go out of her heart ever again. Not even when it is dead. All this the man does not know; he knows nothing. He does not know the difference before love and after love, before motherhood and after motherhood. He can know nothing. Only a woman can know that and speak of that. That is why we won't be told what to do by our husbands.[116]

Every woman, whether she knows it or not, carries "the fruit of the night" in her body. This fruit may not be an actual child; it may be a biological image of the Self—i.e., the child as future potential.

The "known psychic processes" have been, until recently, the product of a male consciousness. But the physiological roots of the processes belong to the feminine modality, and it is probably those physiological roots that were celebrated at Eleusis. Today those mysteries remain in the female body and the woman who takes possession of her body at a conscious level is once again being initiated into them.

Villa of the Mysteries in Pompeii

At the Villa of the Mysteries in Pompeii, eight frescoes reveal the Dionysian initiation of a cultured Roman matron.[117] They are of special interest to us because they picture a woman living in Imperial Rome, in a culture similar to our own, where her feminine nature must have been threatened by her conscious masculine development.

The frescoes are based on the myth of Ariadne, who was betrothed to Dionysus, but forsook him when she fell in love with Theseus, the Athenian sun-hero, and ran away with him. On the island of Naxos, he deserted her as she slept. When she awoke to what had happened, she tried to commit suicide by running into the arms of Death, but Death was in fact Dionysus, who arose from the sea and consummated a love-marriage with her. Thus Ariadne experienced the transforming power of the ecstasy of union with the spirit and at the same time the ecstasy of surrender to the instinctive flow of life.[118]

The initiate probably experienced the mystery of the god in an underground passage of the Villa. This mystery was revealed to her as a divine child in the form of a phallus, a ritual object contained in a winnowing basket, traditionally the crib of the god who was later reborn as the god of instinct and of death and fertility. This mystery symbolized an inner surrender which allowed the woman to experience her deepest erotic potentiality.

Ariadne was the sister of the Minotaur. In her one-sided flight towards consciousness she forsook her own Dionysian Darkness but was sabotaged by the deeper unconscious power within her. Only by giving up all personal desire, and in her total aloneness and despair surrendering to what she believed was Death, did she experience the love-marriage with the god—the coming together of the divine and the human, masculine and feminine—and transformation through that marriage.

Figure 5. The initiate with the winnowing basket.
(Villa of the Mysteries fresco, Pompeii)

Paradoxically, a woman becomes conscious of herself as an individual in a nonpersonal encounter, for in the religious experience she recognizes herself as a part of Life. At the same time, she becomes conscious of the god within her and becomes a mother to him. This surrender to Death is crucial for the woman because everything in her nature demands relatedness to Life, to the man she loves, to her children. To surrender to the spirit seems a rejection of Life, a leap into a black abyss. But it is the sacrifice she must make if she is to find her own god within.

The seventh fresco in the Villa of Mysteries shows the initiate after the overwhelming experience of the mystery in the underground passage (Figure 5, opposite).[119] She kneels as if to uncover the winnowing basket which she seems to have brought back with her, but a black-winged angel intervenes with a whip. This picture seems to reveal a critical moment in a woman's individuation, when her experience of the god within leaves her with an inflation which would allow her to reveal the mystery, but which, once revealed, loses its power and takes on a banal character. An intense experience of the god cannot be shared in words.[120] The phallus definitely suggests that the masculine creative spirit in the woman manifests itself in sexuality, whether in actual physical union, or in the experience of union in her bodily depths. The angel, a feminine Holy Spirit, will not allow her to unveil her secret.

This secret she shares in silence in the eighth fresco. There she kneels in despair with her head in the lap of a previously initiated woman, who keeps her eye on the angel who is about to strike with a whip (Figure 6, page 110). Esther Harding, in *The Parental Image,* says of these last two frescoes:

> On her return to the upper room she must be purged by castigation of all possessiveness regarding the mystery in which she has participated. In this way, she comes to her own true womanhood. This is an emotional experience, not an increase of conscious intellectual understanding as in the case of the man.[121]

What this means, psychologically, is that a woman dare not identify with the archetypal image of the animus, for then she falls into his power and becomes vulnerable to his dark side. Her suffering lies in having known the divine and having it again cut off from her. In accepting her purely human helplessness, she opens herself to redemption. The final stage in the initiation process is embodied by the woman in the last fresco, Figure 9, page 124.

The woman who fails to make this differentiation in the cave of

Figure 6. The initiate in despair, protected by a woman who has been through the process. (Villa of the Mysteries fresco, Pompeii)

Hecate, brings forth the divine child from the fire of the manger and then equates the process with her own rather than an impersonal power working through her. Such a woman becomes "a witch" and is in danger of killing her own child. Because she does not separate the ego from the Self, she falls into inflation. The dead laurel becomes the broomstick of the worst sort, for it is the removed phallus which she claims as her own. When the mother becomes the possessed lover of her infant, she reabsorbs it into her own biological being. Instead of returning to her own humanity, she takes possession of the symbol of her divinity as mother-goddess. The child then becomes a "sacrifice" to her, even as Adonis was sacrificed to Venus, remaining as a vegetation god (unconscious), forever bound to her.

The woman must differentiate herself both from instinct and from spirit; otherwise she will try to possess one or the other and end by being possessed. Once she has experienced the Self, through the recognition and acceptance of the opposites, then she can consciously relax into her own womanhood and allow Life to come to her through her own Being. Life began for Ariadne when she accepted Death—the death of her own personal hopes and longings.

Dance

Modern woman cannot go back to the Dionysian Mysteries, but she must make the journey into the dark regions below, and back again. She, too, must experience that light in her own darkness. Somehow she must again find the sacred mystery within her own body and revere it both as sacred and as a mystery. Dance is one practical way of listening to her body.

One of the women in the experiment found her own Dionysian route when, like Ariadne, she was struck down by a Grace which came to her as overwhelming tragedy. For years she had hoped for a child, but her active animus-driven life gave her no time to relate to her feminine side. At last she conceived and carried her baby for nine months, but he died just before he was born. Her grief was inconsolable, and words were impossible. At first she did not even cry. Then she began analysis and at the same time attended a creative dance class. In her diary she wrote:

> Dance—God, I am lucky to have it! That, more than anything will bring my mind and body together. If the body is the unconscious then perhaps that grief can be danced out of me, just as joy can be expressed.

Dance puts the mind right into the body. It must think and feel every
part of the human being and perhaps in that way it can release or bring
to consciousness the grief within . . . .
I am tangling with the concept of the core of one's being. That is
where my ache is. There is no rational thinking there—it just is. It is
where in T'ai Chi the source of energy originates. It is where in dance
the dancer breathes and gives the movement soul. Oddly enough, it is
also where the foetus grows. I am just starting to identify my centre
again. I remember when I was pregnant I couldn't express myself
through movement. There was no soul—someone else, the baby, had
occupied that core of me. . . . I need to dance because when I dance, I
am. In one gesture I can feel the agony and the joy. In dance, I live.
Where is my centre? Thank God for the dance. I slowly found the
core; the energy and the soul of my dance came back. With the found
physical centre, the dance and my happiness had some substance. And
then, the drawing on inner resources to find the mind's Self. The body
centre, which I consider my real centre, sends the energy up the spine
like a spark to ignite the mind. . . . I become the movement, the agony
disappears and is replaced by joy—a bursting into bloom.
Dance moulds feeling into form. It expresses the experience when
words fail. In dance the rational and intuitive begin to flow freely into
each other. Dance invokes the total body. The dancer bares her soul
totally to the form and feeling. I internalize every move and try to
connect it with breathing. The body moves because it has to in order to
survive. That personal experience of gathering the inner resources into
a full centre gives forth a burst of energy. The agony I feel before dance
disappears—as though life is passing through me. I become a conductor
of the universal spirit. That is the birth process—life passes through me.
That's why the pain goes when I dance, for I create. I become part of
the life force again. The dance is dancing me.

Over a period of eight months the dance brought the young woman
into a deep enough relationship to herself that she was able to accept the following dream as a living sacrifice:

I am standing in bright sunlight. I am holding my baby. He has a
golden knife in his heart. It doesn't seem to bother me that he is
dead. There is no anger. My arms are outstretched as if I am offering
him to God.

She felt no anger because her months of seclusion and grief had
brought her to the realization that her child had to be sacrificed in
order for her own Self to be born.

Intuitively she had felt that the child under her heart was a boy.
Unconsciously, she had projected the meaning of her whole life
onto that child who would redeem her from her feminine instincts
and the overwhelming guilt and fear associated with them. Her
years of being driven by a tyrannical Jehovah culminated in the

sacrifice of her firstborn son. That sacrifice drove her into the arms of Death and into the darkest depths of her own feminine nature where she found the light of her own Being. That light appeared in her dreams in images which exactly paralleled her physical experiences; thus she was able consciously to recognize and integrate the psyche-soma conflict which for so long had kept her barren. She was then able to free her instinctual energy, making it spiritually available as a life force.

As soon as she was able to accept her sacrifice as part of the Grace which brought to birth her own feminine Self, she conceived and bore a girl child. By keeping the balance between psyche and body, she was able to recognize both as divine and to build her own ego in relationship to them, at the same time surrendering her ego demands.

This concept of dance seems to me to be crucial, because although music and dance have been a major part of women's lives from the beginning of time, few modern women, especially intuitives and feeling types, know anything about "becoming the dance." Their highly developed consciousness allows them to enjoy social dancing, but to give themselves up to their emotions and the music and thus experience their own corresponding depths terrifies them. That leap into the unconscious, however, is the very link that could connect them to the life force.

Words are inadequate to express intense passion even when language assumes its most symbolic form. Moreover, words can be dangerous for a woman because they tend to encase her in a personal realm and in a realm of masculine formulation of ideas. The more she talks, the more her inner voice is saying, "No, that's not it at all."

Music transports her into a nonpersonal dimension, a world that speaks directly to her heart, instead of to her head, a world where she can experience wholeness and harmony. Thus she can become aware of her animal nature without becoming identified with it. This is not to recommend that women return to primal dance. Rather it is to suggest that the medium of music and creative dance is one of the surest ways to bring consciousness into the forgotten muscles. The dialogue with one's own body is a form of active imagination.

Dance is a way of bringing offerings of wheaten cakes and honey to the snake beneath the altar, and through this sacrifice bringing release and purification. With a very conscious attitude towards that process, a woman can experience the snake as both begetter and begotten. In dance she can surrender her ego possessiveness and experience her body as a vessel through which divine power can flow. Thus she can experience herself in a totally new way; she is literally transformed. Her own body may become the winnowing basket through which she experiences the mystery. Only then is she free to love, to be the channel through which Eros flows.

Christianity and the Feminine

Women of the 20th century must find those rites which take the form that our present stage of consciousness requires. The archetypes in themselves are timeless and unknowable. What we know directly from experience are the images they assume in time. Though the archetypes remain, the images change and pass. By becoming uprooted from the past through the inevitable decay of its images, we are forced to confront our own experience of ourselves as a mystery. Only through a growing awareness of our own alienation from ourselves do we come to accept the necessity of plunging into apparent chaos. The experience of giving birth to oneself (as the dancer above had to do before she could give birth to her child) is essentially the experience of Demeter, plunging the child into the manger of fire.

Katherine's Crowned Serpent Dream

The dreams of modern women suggest that a new consciousness is imminent. Katherine's serpent dream (in Chapter II) revealed a dark, disconnected force in her psyche. One of her later dreams reveals a transformation in the serpent and the possibility of a new beginning:

> I am in a deep underground cave. Suddenly a serpent appears to me with glowing light crowning its head. I see the crown is a living eye. It weaves merrily through a dark winding passageway and I follow. We come into a stone room with one stone shelf cut into the wall. [Figure 7] Two ancient books are on the shelf. The snake beckons to me to take one. I pick out the closer of the two, entitled *The Seven Chronicles of the Western World,* but when I attempt to open it, the snake strikes my hand with its head. A voice says, "That is finished. The other is for you." I take it in my hands, but I do not open it, for its overwhelming message comes to me through its cover. It is a lavender colour exquisitely etched

Figure 7. The crowned serpent with the two ancient books.
(Original in colour, painted by the dreamer)

with a field of tiny flowers and vines. On the field is a cross from corner to corner and in the centre, one living eye looks into mine. It is as if the wisdom of the ages contained in the book penetrates my very Being through the heart of the eye. I awake, feeling I have been in the presence of the Eighth Eye, the Eye of God. [Figure 8]

This dream suggests a new cycle which may be interpreted both on a personal and collective level. The serpent, acting as psychopomp, guides with its illuminated eye through the darkness to a book which bears the same eye. The black snake carrying the luminous light suggests a reconciliation of opposites, a reconciliation of the chthonic and the spiritual; the illumination is through the darkness of the cave; the new book is covered with garlands and vines.

The snake indicates that divine healing power comes through the second book. *The Seven Chronicles of the Western World* are not for the woman. Does this suggest, on a collective level, that patriarchal consciousness and its rational devotion to material progress has to be transcended? Katherine associated the Eighth Eye with the Book of Revelation (10:4):

And when the seven thunders had uttered their voices, I was about to write: and I heard a voice from heaven saying unto me, "Seal up those things which the seven thunders uttered, and write them not."

The serpent is an earth spirit whose sinuous movement nevertheless keeps a central course. Symbolically, that may be interpreted as a balance of the conscious and unconscious, physically and psychically. In her associations Katherine said:

The world I have been true to—conventional religion, conventional feeling—has kept me locked in my head, compulsively bound to a Jehovah God which I never recognized as such. The serpent is a Christ figure forcing me to break from these compulsions, forcing me to take the responsibility for the new book. Christ came to free us from the law and release us into the spirit, but I never knew what that meant until I felt the power of that Eye. That Presence took all the pressure off of me.

The serpent is in effect the guardian of the "treasure hard to attain." Its Eye seems to hold the secret of her life, connecting her with her own deepest life process. Jung pointed out that "emotions are not detachable like ideas or thoughts, because they are identical with certain physical conditions and are thus deeply rooted in the heavy matter of the body."[122] Through the Eye Katherine is reconnected to those emotions and thus to her body. In this way her spirit is recognized and freed.

Figure 8. The Eighth Eye.
(Original in colour, painted by the dreamer)

The synthesizing power of the unconscious is well illustrated in this dream. The crowned serpent is an androgynous image: the elemental feminine is symbolized by its blackness, but the illuminated crown, the Eye, suggests the masculine psychopomp leading to the transformative Eros in the Eighth Eye. Ultimately her feminine ego is breaking its identification with patriarchal consciousness and finding its conscious relationship to the feminine principle of Eros.

Cultural Implications

For those of us still trying to relate to the roots of our culture through the Christian myth, we must ask ourselves how reconnection with the feminine principle would transform our conscious attitude towards the Christian symbols.

Jung saw the acceptance of the dogma of the Assumption of the Virgin Mary as a crucial step forward in Christianity. Mary, in the view of the Church, performs a function similar to that of Demeter/Persephone in the Eleusinian mysteries. She it is who as a virgin[123] surrenders herself to a nonpersonal power and gives birth to a divine son. She allows her body to be used as the vehicle for conception and birth. This archetypal image is at the centre of the Christmas festival, but for the majority of Christians it is a projected image, and therefore external to themselves. Because they have no experience of the numinous, religion has ceased to hold a central place in their lives. Without the feminine spiritual experience of surrender, conception, and giving birth (both in men and women), the human link which connects us to our deepest psychic roots is missing. It is through the feminine modality that the Incarnation can take place—the spirit can be received and born out of the flesh. Thus the whole personality is transformed through intense emotional response.

This is not the passive acceptance which submits to allowing things to happen—that simply leads to masochistic suffering. Rather it is an open feminine response to a life-affirming moment, a full feminine YES, which requires all one's courage and faith and love to utter. At that moment she is both subject and object, for she voluntarily opens herself to the overshadowing "of the power of the Highest" (Luke 1: 35). The divine son which she bears as a result of that union will fecundate her entire Being.

The woman who has pondered that mystery in her heart will never be merely sprung from Adam's rib, for she has not come to her spirituality through a head trip: she has not merely identified with her positive father-god at the expense of her feminine instinct. This latter kind of spirituality can only leave her essentially cut off from life, from her own feminine, and paradoxically, from her own positive masculinity. Genuine spiritual experience for the woman must penetrate with passion into her body, and her yielding to that power brings forth the new creation, the new attitude to her immediate environment. The immediacy of the moment will demand her flexibility, wisdom and compassion in each daily situation. Reality becomes meaningful through "the intersection of the timeless moment."[124]

In "Women in Europe," first published in 1927, Jung refers to the love of a woman in the following way:

> Her love wants the whole man—not mere masculinity as such but also its negation. The love of woman is not sentiment, as is a man's, but a will that is at times terrifyingly unsentimental and can even force her to self-sacrifice. A man who is loved in this way cannot escape his inferior side, for he can only respond to the reality of her love with his own reality. And this reality is no fair semblance, but a faithful reflection of that eternal human nature which links together all humanity, a reflection of the heights and depths of human life which are common to us all . . . . women are increasingly aware that love alone can give them full stature, just as men are beginning to divine that only the spirit can give life its highest meaning. Both seek a psychic relationship because love needs the spirit, and the spirit love, for its completion. . . . What is down below is not just an excuse for more pleasure, but something we fear because it demands to play its part in the life of the more conscious and complete man.[125]

Woman must heal the inner wounds. For this she needs psychic relationship, which is only possible, according to Jung, "if there is a psychic distance between people, in the same way that morality presupposes freedom."[126] Unrelatedness leads to a feeling of spiritual starvation.

> The feminine psyche responds to this hunger, for it is the function of Eros to unite what Logos has sundered. The woman of today is faced with a tremendous cultural task—perhaps it will be the dawn of a new era. [127]

Events of the past fifty years have proved the reality of Jung's prophecy. Unfortunately, the way to the feminine has too often been by circuitous routes which seek to possess it by laying violent hands upon it. These short cut methods end in violation because the essence of the feminine is its mystery, which we dare not rape by suddenly forcing it into the broad light of the sun. The feminine eventually reveals its dark mystery—at the right time. The period of incubation is now going on in many women who although not join-ing protest groups are nevertheless questioning their "caged" feel-ings in an attempt to find their way to freedom. Jean Baker Miller, writing of women in the 1970s, says:

> In our time we have heard a great deal about people's lack of authen-ticity. What we cannot hear so clearly is that, for half the population, the attempt at authenticity requires a clear and direct risk. For women to act and react out of their own being is to fly in the face of their ap-pointed definition and their prescribed way of living. To move toward authenticity, then, also involves creation, in an immediate and pressing personal way.[128]

What does the opening of the Eighth Eye mean for an understand-ing of the psychology of the obese woman? Jung has argued that for the Western psyche, Christ remains a primary image of the Self and that the loss of that image would have immeasurable consequences.[129] He sees one of the central symbols of Christianity in the crucifixion, which he interpreted as Christ's struggle to differentiate the God image of the Old Testament, a struggle prefigured in the Book of Job.[130] His *Answer to Job* contained within it his analysis of what he considered the distinctive Christian consciousness. The failure to attain that consciousness by distinguishing between the God image in the Old and New Testaments, he suggested, led to a regressive psychology in which the sacrifice of the son was viewed as a willing and necessary submission to the Old Testament God. By refusing to confront the negative aspects of the Old Testament Father, the Christ of orthodox theology (viewed as an archetype) imaged the imprison-ed psyche bound to a positive father complex.[131] What the theolo-gians considered sacrifice becomes in this context psychic murder or, more specifically for this study, psychic suicide.[132]

For Jung, the meaning of Christ as an image of the Self lies in the necessity of living a life as authentic as Christ's own.[133] For the obese woman it means the discovery of her own femininity, which necessarily involves a painful separation from the positive father— through a direct confrontation with his darkness.

The tragedy of the obese woman lies on the one hand in the loss of her own feminine reality, and on the other in her desire to redeem the Father by taking on His darkness without any conscious under-standing of what she is doing. Until she recognizes that it is her own life she is attempting to redeem, she will remain the victim. To realize that it is her own life that is at stake requires of her the recognition that the sins of the parents (both actual and archetypal) cannot be assumed in the form of her own unconscious guilt. Rather she must open her eyes to the darkness within her and assume the responsibility for her own shadow.

Many women are still in the dispensation of the Father because they, like their mothers and grandmothers, have accepted the patriarchal values and rejected their own body, and with it their own shadow. In this way they have avoided the crucifixion, but they have also lost contact with their own personal reality and the possibility of the birth of their own divine child from their own sacred matter. Spiritual birth, like biological birth, requires a union of the opposites, and the sacred child is born from the union of the spirit with the redeemed feminine. In the dispensation of the Father, there is no place for the conscious woman. She is mythically trapped in the dark side through identification, via Eve, with the dark snake.

The healing power of the snake has been overlooked by the Church. When so much emphasis is put on the light side of Christ, the dark side, repressed, takes on demonic proportions. Women, historically, have tended to be identified with that dark side. Their salvation, psychologically, is to live out consciously the psychic process symbolized by the crucifixion. The suffering of the cross involves the recognition of the opposites and the integration of the dark side.[134]

The woman who truly loves must accept the unavoidable suffering of the cross; only consciousness can redeem her from blind misery. That redemption is through a love that transcends her personal desire. The age of the Eighth Eye is surely the coming of the dark, unconscious snake to the light of Eros, to the conscious understanding of love, and the recognition that the instinctual feminine and the transcendent feminine are ultimately One. The age of the Holy Spirit is the age of the reconciliation of opposites.

The dark side of God, associated in Christian theology with the Old Testament Jehovah, who requires the death of his son to appease his wrath and fulfil his primitive sense of justice, makes Satan and Eve at once his foes and allies.[135] Satan is one of the sons of God. In Jungian terms, he constitutes "the fourth," which resolves the Christian trinity into a fourfold consciousness. Eve's identification with Satan in the myth of the Fall gives to the woman the task of restoring Satan to his original form as Lucifer, the Morning Star or light-bringer, which is the form he assumes in the dream of the Eighth Eye.

Without the feminine, Satan and Christ must remain polarized opposites. The feminine is the love that binds the hostile brothers. Ann Ulanov, recognizing the role of the feminine in Christianity, writes:

> ... Contrary to the criticism that Christianity severs the spirit and the flesh, the recognition of the feminine reveals that vital to Christ's love is the sexual polarity which affirms the union of flesh and spirit. Contrary to the criticism that Christianity devalues both ego and aggression, the full recognition of the feminine asserts the proper function of aggression, to serve love. [136]

This suggests that the feminine is the vehicle of the Holy Spirit. In other words, woman is the feminine side of Christ when Christ is recognized in his androgynous nature as the true reconciler enacting within himself the *hieros gamos*.

Consciousness in the Judaic-Christian myth has been too long identified with original sin. Eve, by identifying herself with the serpent and tempting Adam to eat of the tree of knowledge, is in psychic reality offering man consciousness. She thus releases him from the womb of Eden. Eve in this respect gives birth to Adam rather than Adam giving birth to Eve. She gives birth to man, even as Mary gives birth to Christ. In this paradoxical situation, Eve as "temptress" and Eve as the container of the redemptive seed of consciousness, resides the true meaning of the feminine psyche in which the instinctual feminine (the dark, unconscious snake which is at once Satan and man's vegetative nature) and the transcendent feminine (Satan as Lucifer, psychopomp, light-bringer) are one.

In the course of this study, one resolution of obesity has become clear. If the little owl, bewildered and bewitched, rejects her role as the baker's daughter, she can throw off her cloak of many feathers and become "capable of her own distress." Then she can come out from behind the patriarchal eyes and recognize the beggar at her own back door. In that stranger she may discover her own psychological identity with Eve and the Virgin Mary. Her emancipation lies in the psychic enactment of her own physical resurrection—her conscious release from the tomb to which her heritage has unconsciously assigned her, and her entrance into her eternal and divine seed-bearing body.

In the closing stanza of his poem entitled "Among School Children," William Butler Yeats writes:

Labour is blossoming or dancing where
The body is not bruised to pleasure soul,
Nor beauty born out of its own despair,
Nor blear-eyed wisdom out of midnight oil.
O chestnut-tree, great rooted blossomer,
Are you the leaf, the blossom or the bole?
O body swayed to music, O brightening glance,
How can we know the dancer from the dance?

For too long the body has been "bruised to pleasure soul," the feminine nature denied to feed the rational mind. The one-sidedness of extreme spiritualization has produced only a "blear-eyed wisdom" born of "midnight oil." The tree of life does not unfold towards the fruit of individuation in this manner. Consciousness must share in the organic nature of the tree itself. The "brightening glance" of the Eighth Eye, the eye of the healing serpent whose feminine power Christianity has largely ignored, must be allowed to penetrate to its darkest depths. Only then can the "great-rooted blossomer" stretch to its true height, sway to its true music, dance to the One dance.

Figure 9. The final stage in the transition from girlhood to womanhood.
(Villa of the Mysteries fresco, Pompeii)

Notes

CW — *The Collected Works of C.G. Jung*

1. Act IV, sc. v, lines 41-43.
2. *Hamlet*, ed. G.L. Kittridge, pp. 257-258.
3. Neurosis as a form of bewitchment is explored at length by Marie-Louise von Franz in *The Psychological Meaning of Redemption Motifs in Fairytales.*
4. Act IV, sc. vii, lines 168-184.
5. William Butler Yeats, "The Second Coming."
6. For a full discussion of hypercellularity, see Lester B. Salans, "Cellularity of Adipose Tissue," *Treatment and Management of Obesity*, pp. 17-24.
7. Paul B. Beeson and Walsh McDermott, *Textbook of Medicine*, 14th ed., p. 1376.
8. Peter Calow, *Biological Machines: A Cybernetic Approach to Life*, pp. 63-64. "In mammals there is a complex regulatory system centred on the hypothalamus which closely matches energy intake with expenditure. Glucose in the blood binds to cells at the hypothalamic centre and this seems to inhibit the 'urge to feed.' Since carbohydrate reserves are depleted much more between meals than protein or fats this *glucostatic mechanism*, as it is called, provides a coherent account of the day-to-day regulation of energy input. More long-term regulation, however, is effected through a distinct, but related, *lipostatic mechanism.* The latter is thought to inhibit food intake whenever sufficient energy is derived from mobilization of surplus body fat and, because of the intimate association between glucose metabolism and the release of free fatty acids, it may well act through the glucostatic mechanism as well. It is clear, then, that the glucostatic mechanism carries short-term information on 'how the organism is' and the lipostatic mechanism answers the same question on the long-term. Both feed back negatively on the same hypothalamic centre which in turn feeds back positively on the 'urge to feed.'"
9. R.E. Nisbett, "Starvation and the Behaviour of the Obese," *Treatment and Management of Obesity*, p. 47.
10. L.B. Salans, "Cellularity of Adipose Tissue," *Treatment and Management of Obesity*, p. 24.
11. "Flying Saucers: A Modern Myth," CW 10, par. 655.
12. "A Review of the Complex Theory," CW 8, par. 201.
13. Ibid., par. 198.
14. Ibid., par. 204.
15. Ibid., par. 210.
16. According to Jung's model of psychological types, there are two personality attitudes (introversion and extraversion) and four basic functions: sensation, thinking, feeling, and intuition. (Cf. "Definitions," in *Psychological Types*, CW 6) In brief: *sensation* tells us that something exists; *thinking* tells us what it is; *feeling* tells us what it's worth to us; and *intuition* tells us what we can do with it (the possibilities). For practical reasons it is necessary to distinguish feeling—as a rational, judgemental function—from emotion, which comes from an activated complex.

17. *Symbols of Transformation,* CW 5, par. 457.

18. Hilde Bruch, *Eating Disorders,* p. 87.

19. Esther Harding, *Psychic Energy,* pp. 210-211.

20. Hilde Bruch, *Eating Disorders,* p. 127.

21. The relationship of the sex hormones to metabolism has not been established. However, Beeson and McDermott, *Textbook of Medicine,* state: "The relationship between parity and obesity and the frequent menopausal gain in weight, although difficult to document, suggest a possible role of female sex hormones in the regulation of fat metabolism." (p. 1376) This is a possibility worth noting when considering the loss of the feminine in the obesity problem.

22. G. Bray, *International Journal of Obesity* 2, No. 2 (1978), p. 105.

23. Conversations with Rosales Wynne-Roberts, M.D., helped to clarify underlying biochemical mechanisms discussed in this chapter.

24. Jay Tepperman, *Metabolic and Endocrine Physiology,* 3rd ed., p. 201.

25. George F. Cahill, Jr., "Obesity and the Control of Fuel Metabolism," *Treatment and Management of Obesity,* p. 9. Cahill points out in this article that "overweight people need much more insulin. . . . Insulin is the primary controller of the fat cell, telling the fat cell, when adequate fuel is present, to take up the fuel and to store it. . . . In certain situations, particularly in obesity, fat cells need more insulin for each one of the metabolic events it controls. Moreover, other body tissues in the obese individual also need more insulin." For a detailed study of the generalized impairment of insulin action in the tissues of the obese, see Lester B. Salans, "Cellularity of Adipose Tissue," *Treatment and Management of Obesity,* pp. 17-24.

26. Paul B. Beeson and Walsh McDermott, *Textbook of Medicine,* 14th ed., p. 1375.

27. Richard Mackarness, *Eat Fat and Grow Slim,* p.43. Nature can store energy by using two different kinds of carbon-hydrogen bonds. One is the basic structure of fat, the other the basic structure of carbohydrate. Because of the difference between the chemical structures of carbohydrate and fat, carbohydrate yields 4 calories per gram, whereas fat yields 9.4 calories per gram. When carbohydrate is stored, it requires 1.5 grams of water for every gram of glycogen, whereas fat storage requires little increase in intercellular fluid. Therefore, if a cell expands its carbohydrate depot, it is setting up a poor way to store energy, especially when the owner has to carry it around with her.

28. Ibid., p. 45.

29. Ibid., p. 108.

30. Salans points out in "Cellularity of Adipose Tissue" (above, note 6) that many cellular abnormalities have been discovered in the obese individual, but it has also been proved that these are reversible through weight loss. Speculation, therefore, centres on the possibility that "the disordered metabolism of the obese patient can somehow be explained by a resistance to glucose metabolism in the adipose cell."

31. Richard Mackarness, *Not All in the Mind,* p. 38.

32. Ibid., p. 41.

33. E. Cheraskin and W.M. Ringsdorf, Jr., *Psychodietetics,* p. 31.

34. Ibid., p. 73.

35. To further support this theory, the *International Journal of Obesity*, 2, No. 2 (1978), pp. 106-107, reports that "the syndrome of hypothalamic obesity is well established both clinically and experimentally . . . . the most important abnormality in this syndrome is the increased concentration of insulin."

36. Robert C. Atkins, *Dr. Atkins' Diet Revolution*, p. 61. The metabolic changeover effective during Dr. Atkins' diet may be based on a hormone discussed by L. Levin in *Science News Letter* (May 5, 1951). Levin reported on "a new pituitary hormone that appears to act directly instead of through the adrenal glands (as does ACTH). It sets off the body's mechanism for mobilizing fat and the production of the new hormone is set off by the presence of cortisone in the blood." The Council of Foods and Nutrition, reporting on this diet, states that Atkins implies that unlimited amounts of a low carbohydrate ketogenic diet can be eaten without a weight increase, but there is no scientifically acceptable evidence to support this claim. (Council of Foods and Nutrition, Yang and von Itallie, 1976)

37. Hans Selye, *Stress Without Distress*, p. 25.

38. Flanders Dunbar, *Mind and Body*, p. 264.

39. Richard Mackarness, *Not All in the Mind*, p. 108.

40. A.H. Crisp, "Some Aspects of the Relationship between Body Weight and Sexual Behaviour with Particular Reference to Massive Obesity and Anorexia Nervosa," *International Journal of Obesity*, 2, No. 1 (1978), p. 19.

41. In the light of present-day knowledge, adrenin must represent a mixture of hormones from the medulla and cortex of the adrenal gland.

42. Walter Cannon, *Bodily Changes in Pain, Hunger, Fear and Rage*, p. 63.

43. Ibid., pp. 63-64.

44. Ibid., p. 351.

45. Ibid., pp. 194-205. Unless the blood sugar falls below the physiological range of normal, there is not an adrenalin reaction.

46. Ibid., p. 247.

47. Russell A. Lockhart, "Cancer in Myth and Dream," *Spring 1977*, pp. 1-2.

48. From a letter of C.G. Jung to his cousin, Rudolph Jung, May 11, 1956. In *C.G. Jung: Letters*, 2, p. 297.

49. Flanders Dunbar, *Emotions and Bodily Changes*, pp. 260 and 232.

50. Ethan A.H. Sims, "Studies in Human Hyperphagia," *Treatment and Management of Obesity*, p. 35.

51. Ibid., p. 42.

52. J. Tepperman, *Metabolic and Endocrine Physiology*, p. 219.

53. Richard Nisbett, "Starvation and the Behaviour of the Obese," *Treatment and Management of Obesity*, p. 54.

54. J. Tepperman, *Metabolic and Endocrine Physiology*, p. 215.

55. "Investigations with Galvanometer and Pneumograph," CW 2, par. 1062.

56. Ibid., par. 1067.

57. Ibid.

58. Ibid., par. 1080.

59. Ibid., par. 1352.

60. Neither Helen nor Katherine was subject to migraine headache, but the mysterious appearance and disappearance of swelling under stress has been well documented. "Before the onset of migraine headache a generalized accumulation of fluid may occur as part of a non-specific disturbance in fluid and electrolytes that is found in many persons with and without the migraine syndrome during periods of stress. There is evidence of a general abnormality of vascular behaviour in many migraine subjects." Beeson and McDermott, *Textbook of Medicine*, p. 617.

61. "On the Nature of the Psyche", CW 8, par. 366.

62. Ibid.

63. Ibid., par. 368.

64. Ibid., par. 369.

65. Ibid., par. 375.

66. Ibid., par. 377.

67. Ibid., par. 379.

68. Ibid., par. 380.

69. Cf. note 60 above.

70. "On the Nature of the Psyche," CW 8, par. 407.

71. Ibid., par. 414.

72. Ibid., par. 417.

73. Ibid., pars. 418, 420.

74. *Shadow and Evil in Fairytales*, pp. 215-216.

75. Hilde Bruch, *Eating Disorders*, p. 102.

76. "Association, Dream, and Hysterical Symptom," CW 2, par. 833.

77. Ibid., par. 861.

78. C.G. Jung, "Psychological Aspects of the Mother Archetype," CW 9, I, par. 186.

79. Ibid., par. 184.

80. "Adonais."

81. Hilde Bruch, *The Golden Cage*, p. 34.

82. Keats, "Ode to a Nightingale."

83. *Apuleius' Golden Ass*, p. VIII-10.

84. With reference to the *Rex marinus*, Jung writes: "In reality it is the secret transformative substance, which fell from the highest place into the darkest depths of matter where it awaits deliverance. But no one will plunge into these depths in order, by his own transformation in the darkness and by the torment of fire, to rescue his king. They cannot hear the voice of the king and think it is the chaotic roar of destruction. The sea (*mare nostrum*) of the alchemists is their own darkness, the unconscious. . . . The dark background of the soul contains not only evil but a king in need of, and capable of, redemption." (*Alchemical Studies*, CW 13, par. 183)

85. Esther Harding, *Woman's Mysteries*, p. 266.

86. *Apuleius' Golden Ass*, p. IV-6.

87. Discussed in conversation with Dr.med. A. Ziegler, Zürich.

88. Cf. C.G. Jung, "Flying Saucers: A Modern Myth," CW 10, par. 780: "We now know that a factor exists which mediates between the apparent incommensurability of body and psyche, giving matter a kind of 'psychic' faculty and the psyche a kind of 'materiality,' by means of which the one can work on the other. That the body can work on the psyche seems to be a truism, but strictly speaking all we know is that any bodily defect or illness expresses itself psychically."

89. "Rex and Regina," CW 14, pars. 357f.

90. Ibid., par. 358.

91. C.G. Jung, *Symbols of Transformation*, CW 5, par. 438.

92. Albert Stunkard, "New Treatments for Obesity," *Treatment and Management of Obesity*, p. 104. It is estimated that in general no more than 25% of obese persons lose 20 pounds, and no more than 5% lose 40 pounds.

93. In conversation with a colleague, I learned that Hannah Green, author of *I Never Promised You a Rose Garden*, suffered from obesity, yet she never mentioned this problem in her book, nor was she pictured as obese in the film. This seems a striking example of the modern willingness to reveal the agony of the soul, but at the same time to hide the "shameful" truth of the obese body. A similar reticence appeared in the Association Experiments.

94. James Hillman describes the two sides of this archetype in "Senex and Puer: An Aspect of the Historical and Psychological Present," *Eranos-Jahrbuch*, XXXVI, 1967.

95. M.-L. von Franz, *Apuleius' Golden Ass*, p. IV-5.

96. Diagram patterned from Jung's diagram of the archetype of the marriage quaternio in "The Psychology of the Transference," CW 16, par. 422.

97. Maximilian Rudwin, *The Devil in Legend and Literature*, p. 234ff.

98. John Milton, *Paradise Lost*, IV, line 299.

99. Hilde Bruch, *Eating Disorders*, p. 337.

100. Erich Neumann, *The Child*, pp. 90-91.

101. Ibid., summarized from pp. 105-109.

102. Cf. M.-L. von Franz, *Redemption Motifs in Fairytales*, p. 54-55, regarding projection of the Self onto death, which may be a psychological factor in suicide.

103. *The Feminine in Jungian Psychology and in Christian Theology*, pp. 85-86.

104. CW 18, par. 627.

105. Ibid., par. 632.

106. Ibid., par. 635.

107. Mary Daly, *Beyond God the Father*, p. 43.

108. "The Psychological Aspects of the Kore," CW 9, I, par. 355.

109. See above, note 89.

110. For a full discussion of the androgynous Dionysus, see James Hillman, "First Adam, then Eve," *Eranos-Jahrbuch*, XXXVIII, 1969.

111. C.G. Jung and C. Kerényi, *Introduction to a Science of Mythology*, p. 117.

112. Ibid., p. 144.

113. Ibid., p. 148.

114. From a letter to Pastor Walter Bernet, June 13, 1955, in *C.G. Jung: Letters*, 2, pp. 258-259.

115. "The Psychology of the Child Archetype," CW 9, I, par. 291.

116. Jung and Kerényi, *Introduction to a Science of Mythology*, p. 101.

117. Linda Fierz-David has discussed the psychological significance of these frescoes in *Psychologische Betrachtungen zu der Freskenfolge der Villa dei Misteri in Pompeji*. Unfortunately, this book has not yet been published in English translation.

118. For a fuller discussion of this myth, see C. Kerényi, *Dionysus*.

119. The frescoes are reproduced in C.G. Jung, *Man and His Symbols*, pp. 142-143, where they are discussed by Joseph Henderson.

120. The danger of inflation or identification with a mood is dealt with in the Eleusinian Mysteries through Baubo, whose ribald sense of humour (exposing her buttocks) breaks the spell of Demeter's grief. The grossly human can release vital energy in a woman.

121. Esther Harding, *The Parental Image*, pp. 34-35.

122. "The Tavistock Lectures," CW 18, par. 317.

123. For a full discussion of the meaning of "virgin," see Esther Harding, *Woman's Mysteries*, pp. 146-149.

124. Eliot, *Four Quartets*, "Little Gidding."

125. CW 10, pars 261, 269, 271.

126. Ibid., par. 273.

127. Ibid., par. 275.

128. *Toward a New Psychology of Women*, p. 119.

129. *Symbols of Transformation*, CW 5, par. 576.

130. *Answer to Job*, p. 70.

131. Ibid., p. 78.

132. Ibid., p. 91-92.

133. Discussed in a letter to Dorothee Hoch, July 3, 1952, *Letters*, 2, pp. 76-78.

134. C.G. Jung, *Answer to Job*, p. 90: "Why this inevitable result of Christian psychology should signify redemption is difficult to see, except that the conscious recognition of the opposites, painful though it may be at the moment, does bring with it a definite feeling of deliverance. . . . It is on the one hand a deliverance from the distressing state of dull and helpless unconsciousness, and on the other hand a growing awareness of God's oppositeness, in which man can participate if he does not shrink from being wounded by the dividing sword which is Christ. Only in the most extreme and most menacing conflict does the Christian experience deliverance into divinity, always provided that he does not break, but accepts the burden of being marked out by God. In this way alone can the *imago Dei* realize itself in him, and God become a man."

135. Ibid., p. 111.

136. *The Feminine*, p. 313.

Glossary of Jungian Terms

Anima (Latin, "soul"). The unconscious, feminine side of a man's personality. She is personified in dreams by images of women ranging from prostitute and seductress to spiritual guide (Wisdom). She is the Eros principle, hence a man's anima development is reflected in how he relates to women. Identification with the anima can appear as moodiness, effeminacy, and oversensitivity.

Animus (Latin, "spirit"). The unconscious, masculine side of a woman's personality. He personifies the Logos principle. Identification with the animus can cause a woman to become rigid, opinionated, and argumentative. More positively, he is the inner man who acts as a bridge between the woman's ego and her own creative resources in the unconscious.

Archetypes. Irrepresentable in themselves, but their effects appear in consciousness as the archetypal images and ideas. These are collective universal patterns or motifs which come from the collective unconscious and are the basic content of religions, mythologies, legends, and fairytales. They emerge in individuals through dreams and visions.

Association. A spontaneous flow of interconnected thoughts and images around a specific idea, determined by unconscious connections.

Complex. An emotionally charged group of ideas or images. At the "center" of a complex is an archetype or archetypal image.

Constellate. Whenever there is a strong emotional reaction to a person or a situation, a complex has been constellated (activated).

Ego. The central complex in the field of consciousness. A strong ego can relate objectively to activated contents of the unconscious (i.e., other complexes), rather than identifying with them, which appears as a state of possession.

Feeling. One of the four psychic functions. It is a rational function which evaluates the worth of relationships and situations. Feeling must be distinguished from emotion, which is due to an activated complex.

Individuation. The conscious realization of one's unique psychological reality, including both strengths and limitations. It leads to the experience of the Self as the regulating center of the psyche.

Inflation. A state in which one has an unrealistically high or low (negative inflation) sense of identity. It indicates a regression of consciousness into unconsciousness, which typically happens when the ego takes too many unconscious contents upon itself and loses the faculty of discrimination.

Intuition. One of the four psychic functions. It is the irrational function which tells us the possibilities inherent in the present. In contrast to sensation (the function which perceives immediate reality through the physical senses) intuition perceives via the unconscious, e.g., flashes of insight of unknown origin.

Participation mystique. A term derived from the anthropologist Lévy-Bruhl, denoting a primitive, psychological connection with objects, or between persons, resulting in a strong unconscious bond.

Puella aeternae (Latin, "eternal girl"). Indicates a certain type of woman who remains too long in adolescent psychology, generally associated with a strong unconscious attachment to the father. Her male counterpart is the puer aeternus, an "eternal youth" with a corresponding tie to the mother.

Persona (Latin, "actor's mask"). One's social role, derived from the expectations of society and early training. A strong ego relates to the outside world through a flexible persona; identification with a specific persona (doctor, scholar, artist, etc.) inhibits psychological development.

Projection. The process whereby an unconscious quality or characteristic of one's own is perceived and reacted to in an outer object or person. Projection of the anima or animus onto a real woman or man is experienced as falling in love. Frustrated expectations indicate the need to withdraw projections, in order to be able to relate to the reality of other people.

Self. The archetype of wholeness and the regulating center of the personality. It is experienced as a transpersonal power which transcends the ego, e.g., God.

Shadow. An unconscious part of the personality characterized by traits and attitudes which the conscious ego tends to reject. It is personified in dreams by persons of the same sex as the dreamer.

Symbol. The best possible expression for something essentially unknown. Symbolic thinking is non-linear, right-brain oriented; it is complementary to logical, linear, left-brain thinking.

Transcendent function. The reconciling "third" which emerges from the unconscious (in the form of a symbol or a new attitude) after the opposites have been differentiated, and the tension between them held.

Transference and counter-transference. Particular cases of projection, commonly used to describe the unconscious, emotional bonds that arise between two persons in an analytic or therapeutic relationship.

Uroborus. The mythical snake or dragon that eats its own tail. It is a symbol both for individuation as a self-contained, circular process, and for narcissistic self-absorption.

Bibliography

Atkins, Robert, M.D. *Dr. Atkins' Diet Revolution.* New York: Bantam Books, 1977.

Bray, George, M.D. "Definition, Measurement, and Classification of the Syndromes of Obesity," *International Journal of Obesity,* 2, No. 2 (1978). Ed. Howard and Bray. London: Newton Publ. Ltd., 1978.

Bruch, Hilde, M.D. *The Golden Cage: The Enigma of Anorexia Nervosa.* London: Open Books Publ. Ltd., 1978.

_____. *Eating Disorders: Obesity, Anorexia Nervosa, and the Person Within.* New York: Basic Books Ltd., 1973.

Calow, Peter. *Biological Machines: A Cybernetic Approach to Life.* London: Edward Arnold Ltd., 1976.

Cannon, Walter, M.D. *Bodily Changes in Pain, Hunger, Fear, and Rage.* Boston: Charles T. Branford Co., 1953.

Cheraskin, E., M.D. and Ringsdorf, W.M. Jr., M.D. *Psychodietetics.* New York: Bantam Books, 1974.

C.G. Jung Speaking. Ed. William McGuire and R.F.C. Hull. Princeton: Princeton U.P. (Bollingen Series XCVII), 1977.

Crisp, A.H. "Some Aspects of the Relationship between Body Weight and Sexual Behaviour with Particular Reference to Massive Obesity and Anorexia Nervosa," *International Journal of Obesity,* 2, No. 1, 1978.

Daly, Mary. *Beyond God the Father: Toward a New Philosophy of Women's Liberation.* Boston: Beacon Press, 1977.

Dunbar, Flanders, M.D. *Emotions and Bodily Changes.* New York: Columbia U.P., 1954.

_____. *Mind and Body: Psychosomatic Medium.* New York: Random House, 1947.

Eliot, T.S. *Four Quartets.* London: Faber & Faber, 1952.

Fierz-David, Linda. *Psychologische Betrachtungen zu der Freskenfolge der Villa dei Misteri in Pompeji.* Zürich, 1957.

Graham, Martha. *The Notebooks of Martha Graham.* New York: Harcourt Brace, Jovanovich Inc., 1973.

Harding, Esther. *Psychic Energy: Its Source and Goal.* Washington, D.C.: Publ. for Bollingen Foundation Inc. by Pantheon Books Inc., 1947.

_____. *The Parental Image: Its Injury and Reconstruction.* New York: G.P. Putnam's Sons for C.G. Jung Foundation for Analytical Psychology, 1965.

_____. *Woman's Mysteries.* London: Longmans, Green & Co., 1935.

Hillman, James. "Senex and Puer: An Aspect of the Historical and Psychological Present." *Eranos-Jahrbuch, XXXVI,* 1967.

_____. "First Adam, then Eve." *Eranos-Jahrbuch, XXXVIII,* 1969.

Jung, C.G. *The Collected Works* (Bollingen Series XX), 20 vols. Transl. R.F.C. Hull, ed. H. Read, M. Fordham, G. Adler, Wm. McGuire. Princeton: Princeton, U.P., 1953-1979.

_____. *Answer to Job.* Transl. R.F.C. Hull. London: Routledge & Kegan Paul, 1964.

133

_____. *Man and His Symbols.* London: Aldus Books, 1964.

_____. *Letters* (Bollingen Series XCV), 2 vols. Ed. G. Adler. Princeton: Princeton, U.P., 1973-1975.

_____. and Kerényi, Carl. *Introduction to a Science of Mythology: The Myth of the Divine Child and the Mysteries of Eleusis.* Transl. R.F.C. Hull. London: Routledge & Kegan Paul, 1969.

Kerényi, Carl. *Dionysos, Archetypal Image of Indestructible Life.* (Bollingen Series LXV-2). Transl. Ralph Manheim. Princeton: Princeton U.P., 1976.

_____. *The Gods of the Greeks.* Transl. Norman Cameron. London: Thames & Hudson, 1976.

Kittridge, G.L., ed. *Shakespeare's Hamlet.* London, Ginn and Co. (no date).

Lockhart, Russell A. "Cancer in Myth and Dream," *Spring 1977.* Zurich: Spring Publications, 1977.

Mackarness, Richard, M.D. *Eat Fat and Grow Slim.* Glasgow: William Collins Sons & Co. Ltd., 1976.

_____. *Not All in the Mind.* London: Pan Books Ltd., 1977.

Miller, Jean Baker. *Toward a New Psychology of Women,* Aylesbury, England: Penguin Books Ltd., 1976.

Neumann, Erich. *The Child.* New York: G.P. Putnam's Sons for C.G. Jung Foundation for Analytical Psychology, 1973.

Penguin Book of English Verse, ed. John Hayward. London: Penguin Books, 1960.

Rudwin, Maximilian. *The Devil in Legend and Literature.* La Salle, Illinois: The Open Court Publ. Co., 1931.

Selye, Hans, M.D. *Stress Without Distress.* Scarborough: The New American Library of Canada Ltd., 1975.

Tepperman, Jay, M.D. *Metabolic and Endocrine Physiology,* 3rd ed. Chicago: Year Book Medical Publishers Inc., 1974.

Textbook of Medicine, 14th ed. Ed. Paul B. Beeson and Walsh McDermott. Philadelphia: Saunders Publications, 1975.

Treatment and Management of Obesity. Ed. Bray, M.D. and Bethune, M.D. Hagerstown, Maryland: Harper & Row, Medical Department, 1974.

Ulanov, Ann Belford. *The Feminine in Jungian Psychology and in Christian Theology.* Evanston: Northwestern U.P., 1971.

Von Franz, Marie-Louise. *Apuleius' Golden Ass.* Zurich: Spring Publications, 1970.

_____. *The Psychological Meaning of Redemption Motifs in Fairytales.* Toronto: Inner City Books, 1980.

_____. *Shadow and Evil in Fairytales.* Zurich: Spring Publications, 1974.

Index

44. The Dream Story
Donald Broadribb (Baker's Hill, Australia). ISBN 0-919123-45-7. 256 pp. $20

45. The Rainbow Serpent: Bridge to Consciousness
Robert L. Gardner (Toronto). ISBN 0-919123-46-5. 128 pp. $16

46. Circle of Care: Clinical Issues in Jungian Therapy
Warren Steinberg (New York). ISBN 0-919123-47-3. 160 pp. $16

47. Jung Lexicon: A Primer of Terms & Concepts
Daryl Sharp (Toronto). ISBN 0-919123-48-1. 160 pp. $16

48. Body and Soul: The Other Side of Illness
Albert Kreinheder (Los Angeles). ISBN 0-919123-49-X. 112 pp. $16

49. Animus Aeternus: Exploring the Inner Masculine
Deldon Anne McNeely (Lynchburg, VA). ISBN 0-919123-50-3. 192 pp. $18

50. Castration and Male Rage: The Phallic Wound
Eugene Monick (Scranton, PA). ISBN 0-919123-51-1. 144 pp. $16

51. Saturday's Child: Encounters with the Dark Gods
Janet O. Dallett (Seal Harbor, WA). ISBN 0-919123-52-X. 128 pp. $16

52. The Secret Lore of Gardening: Patterns of Male Intimacy
Graham Jackson (Toronto). ISBN 0-919123-53-8. 160 pp. $16

53. The Refiner's Fire: Memoirs of a German Girlhood
Sigrid R. McPherson (Los Angeles). ISBN 0-919123-54-6. 208 pp. $18

54. Transformation of the God-Image: Jung's *Answer to Job*
Edward F. Edinger (Los Angeles). ISBN 0-919123-55-4. 144 pp. $16

55. Getting to Know You: The Inside Out of Relationship
Daryl Sharp (Toronto). ISBN 0-919123-56-2. 128 pp. $16

56. A Strategy for a Loss of Faith: Jung's Proposal
John P. Dourley (Ottawa). ISBN 0-919123-57-0. 144 pp. $16

57. Close Relationships: Family, Friendship, Marriage
Eleanor Bertine (New York). ISBN 0-919123-58-9. 160 pp. $16

58. Conscious Femininity: Interviews with Marion Woodman
Introduction by Marion Woodman (Toronto). ISBN 0-919123-59-7. 160 pp. $16

59. The Middle Passage: From Misery to Meaning in Midlife
James Hollis (Houston). ISBN 0-919123-60-0. 128 pp. $16

60. The Living Room Mysteries: Patterns of Male Intimacy, Book 2
Graham Jackson (Toronto). ISBN 0-919123-61-9. 144 pp. $16

61. Chicken Little: The Inside Story *(A Jungian Romance)*
Daryl Sharp (Toronto). ISBN 0-919123-62-7. 128 pp. $16

62. Coming To Age: The Croning Years and Late-Life Transformation
Jane R. Prétat (Providence, RI). ISBN 0-919123-63-5. 144 pp. $16

63. Under Saturn's Shadow: The Wounding and Healing of Men
James Hollis (Houston). ISBN 0-919123-64-3. 144 pp. $16

Studies in Jungian Psychology
by Jungian Analysts

Quality Paperbacks

Prices and payment in $US (except in Canada, $Cdn)

1. The Secret Raven: Conflict and Transformation
Daryl Sharp (Toronto). ISBN 0-919123-00-7. 128 pp. $16

2. The Psychological Meaning of Redemption Motifs in Fairy Tales
Marie-Louise von Franz (Zürich). ISBN 0-919123-01-5. 128 pp. $16

3. On Divination and Synchronicity: The Psychology of Meaningful Chance
Marie-Louise von Franz (Zürich). ISBN 0-919123-02-3. 128 pp. $16

4. The Owl Was a Baker's Daughter: Obesity, Anorexia and the Repressed Feminine Marion Woodman (Toronto). ISBN 0-919123-03-1. 144 pp. $16

5. Alchemy: An Introduction to the Symbolism and the Psychology
Marie-Louise von Franz (Zürich). ISBN 0-919123-04-X. 288 pp. $20

6. Descent to the Goddess: A Way of Initiation for Women
Sylvia Brinton Perera (New York). ISBN 0-919123-05-8. 112 pp. $16

7. The Psyche as Sacrament: A Comparative Study of C.G. Jung and Paul Tillich John P. Dourley (Ottawa). ISBN 0-919123-06-6. 128 pp. $16

8. Border Crossings: Carlos Castaneda's Path of Knowledge
Donald Lee Williams (Boulder). ISBN 0-919123-07-4. 160 pp. $16

9. Narcissism and Character Transformation: The Psychology of Narcissistic Character Disorders
Nathan Schwartz-Salant (New York). ISBN 0-919123-08-2. 192 pp. $18

10. Rape and Ritual: A Psychological Study
Bradley A. Te Paske (Santa Barbara). ISBN 0-919123-09-0. 160 pp. $16

11. Alcoholism and Women: The Background and the Psychology
Jan Bauer (Montreal). ISBN 0-919123-10-4. 144 pp. $16

12. Addiction to Perfection: The Still Unravished Bride
Marion Woodman (Toronto). ISBN 0-919123-11-2. 208 pp. $18pb/$25hc

13. Jungian Dream Interpretation: A Handbook of Theory and Practice
James A. Hall, M.D. (Dallas). ISBN 0-919123-12-0. 128 pp. $16

14. The Creation of Consciousness: Jung's Myth for Modern Man
Edward F. Edinger (Los Angeles). ISBN 0-919123-13-9. 128 pp. $16

15. The Analytic Encounter: Transference and Human Relationship
Mario Jacoby (Zürich). ISBN 0-919123-14-7. 128 pp. $16

16. Change of Life: Dreams and the Menopause
Ann Mankowitz (Ireland). ISBN 0-919123-15-5. 128 pp. $16

17. The Illness That We Are: A Jungian Critique of Christianity
John P. Dourley (Ottawa). ISBN 0-919123-16-3. 128 pp. $16

18. Hags and Heroes: A Feminist Approach to Jungian Psychotherapy with Couples Polly Young-Eisendrath (Philadelphia). ISBN 0-919123-17-1. 192 pp. $18

19. Cultural Attitudes in Psychological Perspective
Joseph L. Henderson, M.D. (San Francisco). ISBN 0-919123-18-X. 128 pp. $16

20. The Vertical Labyrinth: Individuation in Jungian Psychology
Aldo Carotenuto (Rome). ISBN 0-919123-19-8. 144 pp. $16

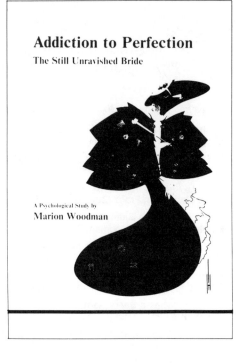

Addiction to Perfection

The Still Unravished Bride

A Psychological Study by
Marion Woodman

12. Addiction to Perfection: The Still Unravished Bride.
Marion Woodman (Toronto). ISBN 0-919123-11-2. 208 pp.

"This book is about taking the head off an evil witch." With these words Marion Woodman begins her spiral journey, a powerful and authoritative look at the psychology and attitudes of modern woman.

The witch is a Medusa or a Lady Macbeth, an archetypal pattern functioning autonomously in women, petrifying their spirit and inhibiting their development as free and creatively receptive individuals. Much of this, according to the author, is due to a cultural one-sidedness that favors patriarchal values—productivity, goal orientation, intellectual excellence, spiritual perfection, etc.—at the expense of more earthy, interpersonal values that have traditionally been recognized as the heart of the feminine.

Marion Woodman's first book, *The Owl Was a Baker's Daughter: Obesity, Anorexia Nervosa and the Repressed Feminine,* focused on the psychology of eating disorders and weight disturbances.

Here, with a broader perspective on the same general themes, she continues her remarkable exploration of women's mysteries through case material, dreams, literature and mythology, in food rituals, rape symbolism, Christianity, imagery in the body, sexuality, creativity and relationships.

"It is like finding the loose end in a knotted mass of thread. . . . What a relief! Somebody knows!"—**Elizabeth Strahan,** *Psychological Perspectives.*

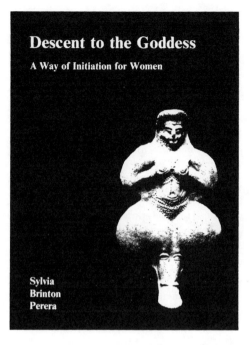

Descent to the Goddess

A Way of Initiation for Women

Sylvia
Brinton
Perera

6. Descent to the Goddess: A Way of Initiation for Women.
Sylvia Brinton Perera (New York). ISBN 0-919123-05-8. 112 pp.

A highly original and provocative book about women's freedom and the need for an inner, female authority in a masculine-oriented society.

Combining ancient texts and modern dreams, the author, a practising Jungian analyst, presents a way of feminine initiation. Inanna-Ishtar, Sumerian Goddess of Heaven and Earth, journeys into the underworld to Ereshkigal, her dark "sister," and returns. So modern women must descend from their old role-determined behavior into the depths of their instinct and image patterns, to find anew the Great Goddess and restore her values to modern culture.

Men too will be interested in this book, both for its revelations of women's essential nature and for its implications in terms of their own inner journey.

"The most significant contribution to an understanding of feminine psychology since Esther Harding's *The Way of All Women*."—**Marion Woodman,** Jungian analyst and author of *Addiction to Perfection, The Pregnant Virgin* and *The Owl Was a Baker's Daughter.*